THE
DEBT-FREE
LIFESTYLE

THE
DEBT-FREE
LIFESTYLE

A STRATEGY FOR THE AVERAGE CANADIAN

CHRISTINE CONWAY

BARLOW BOOKS
fine books for enterprising authors

Library and Archives Canada Cataloguing in Publication data available upon request.

ISBN 978-1-988025-07-0 (paperback)
ISBN 978-1-988025-08-7 (ebook)

Printed in Canada

TO ORDER:
In Canada:
Georgetown Publications
34 Armstrong Avenue, Georgetown, ON L7G 4R9

In the U.S.A.:
Midpoint Book Sales & Distribution
27 West 20th Street, Suite 1102, New York, NY 10011

Publisher: Sarah Scott
Project manager: Zoja Popovic
Managing editor at large: Tracy Bordian
Cover design: Soapbox Design
Interior design: Kyle Gell Design
Page layout: Kyle Gell Design
Copy editing: Heather Sangster / Strong Finish Editorial Design
Proofreading: Strong Finish Editorial Design
Marketing & publicity: Ann Gibbon

For more information, visit **www.barlowbooks.com**

BARLOW BOOKS

Barlow Book Publishing Inc.
96 Elm Avenue, Toronto, ON
Canada M4W 1P2

To my wonderful husband, Cameron Conway. Thank you for going on this crazy adventure with me and enduring the long evenings and weekends while I studied and worked. Thank you for being a constant source of support. Knowing that you will love me whether I succeed or fail has given me the courage to try. You make every day more fun, and you are the best part of my life.

To my mentors, but more importantly my friends, Dave Terpening and Rosalie Leischner. You saw my potential long before I could see it in myself, and the opportunity you provided me with through Braun Financial Services Ltd. has forever changed my life. I am eternally grateful and credit any success I achieve to you. Thank you for your sense of humour, your patience, and for making it fun to come to the office every day. I couldn't have asked for a better career, and I am so glad that I got to spend the past seven years of my life with the both of you. To many more great memories!

contents

OUR STORY

HUMBLE BEGINNINGS

It was a hot summer in Winnipeg, Manitoba, in 2008 when my husband, Cameron, and I decided to move a few provinces west to the Lower Mainland of British Columbia. We were in our mid-twenties and at the beginning of our careers. It was the perfect time to take a risk and leave our family and friends to start fresh in what we viewed as the land of opportunity. The day we arrived, we had no jobs, no support network, and a line of credit that had grown to $10,000. Since then we have managed to pay off our consumer debt, buy a home, and six years after that pay more than $150,000 toward our mortgage. We began our debt-free journey with a combined family income of $78,000 annually. A few short years later, Statistics Canada released its 2011 National Household Survey, which showed a median family income of $76,000 annually across the country.[1] Average as we were, we had chosen to move to one of the most expensive regions in the country, learning pretty quickly that our dollar didn't go as far here as it did in the prairies.

When we lived in Winnipeg, I worked at a managing general agency—an intermediary between independent financial advisors who are contracted with a number of different insurance companies and the insurance companies they represent—for just over $10 an hour. It was an administrative job involving a lot of paperwork, but I learned how to process investments and life insurance applications. Cam had landed a job as a rural and suburban mail carrier replacement worker with Canada Post, filling in for other carriers while they were off work. He sorted and delivered mail to the community post office boxes that Canada Post had been installing in neighbourhoods and condo complexes. Before that, he worked at a windshield washer fluid manufacturer and as a baggage handler and a delivery driver. We were married in our early twenties. I was fresh out of university with my newly minted bachelor of arts in the business track. Cam's college fund was primarily invested in U.S. energy stocks, including Enron, and following the 2001–02 scandal and crash his registered education savings plan (RESP) was worth only 10% of its original value. He was left with nearly nothing saved and had to choose between continuing on to post-secondary education and going into debt or going to work. He chose to work.

Beginning our new life together without any other resources, we spent the first year of marriage living in Cam's grandfather's basement because he was kind enough to let us stay rent-free so we could get on our feet. We had dreams but no plans to get there and, ultimately, no idea where to begin. Our rent-free living had allowed for some savings that first year, but we knew this advantage wouldn't continue once we were out in the real world. Since even my bachelor's degree hadn't prepared me for day-to-day life and managing my finances, I looked to the advisors where I worked. They held in their hands the greatest responsibility: to show others how they could reach their financial goals, to help them find freedom from debt, and to guide them toward a comfortable retirement. Their ability to serve their clients was directly related to the amount of experience and skill they had amassed over the years. I determined then and there, six months into my first real job, that I would become one of those advisors and that my life would be a model for the lessons I would teach others. I enrolled for the first course in the Certified Financial Planner® (CFP®) designation program and started what would be four years of working during the day and studying at night.

Fast-forward a few years to our move to British Columbia in 2008. It took a couple months for me to find a job; fortunately, Cam was able to continue as a Canada Post replacement worker right away. I began working at another managing general agency, making $35,000 annually, and within a year I passed my final exam and became a CFP Professional in 2009. When I was offered an entry-level financial planning job, I was making $40,000 annually. Cameron was eventually hired full-time on a route, making $38,000 annually. Together, our little two-person family was bringing in $78,000 that year.

THE LAND OF OPPORTUNITY IS ... EXPENSIVE

One of the first things we experienced after moving to Metro Vancouver was that the cost of living in British Columbia was much higher than in Winnipeg. Our limited income brought us close to the line and we felt it. Paycheque-to-paycheque living is every bit as awful as it sounds. We had big dreams to buy a home, cars, and save for a comfortable future, but with a small budget it seemed impossible since every dollar we made disappeared as soon as it was earned. Cameron would get a small pension if he stayed with Canada Post, but I wouldn't get one at all. Since there wasn't going to be any more money coming in, the way that we structured our finances was going to make all the difference. But how could we accomplish all that we dreamed of?

We were introduced to the concept of the *living wage*, which answers the affordability question: how much income does an average family of four need to earn to meet the bare minimum requirements of life in their particular region? This includes housing, food, transportation, clothing, and childcare. It doesn't factor in any debt repayment, home ownership costs, or much by the way of savings and entertainment. Since affordability varies with location, if that family wanted to live in the Metro Vancouver area, both parents would each need to be working for at least $20.68 an hour with a 35-hour work week, or $37,638 each annually.[2] While Cam and I weren't a family of four, we still felt the strain, and we quickly found that we needed a way to organize our finances that would not only help us get ahead but also take into account affordability. We were average in every way but had one advantage: I had become a CFP Professional in 2009 and have since been working with clients at an independent financial planning firm. Our personal circumstances as well as the client discussions I've had throughout the years led to the creation of a system that has been tested thoroughly in my own life. *The Debt-Free Lifestyle* represents that system and is a unique book because it is my story both as an advisor and as someone who is facing all the challenges of our generation. It has the potential to change the lives and financial futures of those who chose to implement it.

CONVENTIONAL WISDOM SAYS: JUST MAKE MORE MONEY!

During the day at my office I was having conversations with people—regular people—about their finances. With new clients, it seemed that time after time everyone was facing the

same struggles. People would come to us in their early fifties with their kids mostly grown, the mortgage half paid, a
substantial amount of personal debt, and little savings for
retirement. In many cases, people were completely reliant on
their employer's pension plan to take the burden of retirement savings, and very few knew if what they were doing
was enough. Those who didn't have a pension plan were
even more worried, as they looked at their large debt and
small savings and wondered if they could ever stop working.
Perhaps the bigger issue was that many of them couldn't see
how they could do more with the income they had. There
was always too much month and not enough money. The
stress of an unexpected expense or emergency was enormous
because there wasn't a quick and easy way to get money
except from another credit card. Often, the classic financial
planning advice is to work more, or work harder, and while
that's great advice when it works, it's not always an option.

In our case, at first Cam didn't qualify for overtime at
Canada Post and work wasn't guaranteed because he was a
contractor, but a year later he got his own route and joined
the union. However, because he was designated as a rural
and suburban mail carrier and not a letter carrier, he was
paid substantially less than what many of his coworkers
made for doing the same job. He was also still ineligible
for paid overtime on his route. Similarly, I had agreed to a
fixed salary and my work didn't lean toward overtime either.
I could earn extra income if I could find new clients and sell

product, but I tended to shy away from trying to sell to my clients in favour of trying to educate them instead. While my approach led to a lot of happy customers, I didn't make much extra money. There was no easy way for us to earn additional income, outside of getting second jobs.

We saw that people around us were having the same issues. Some were already working two jobs and didn't know how to give any more time or energy to earning income. Others had young kids at home, and while getting things in order financially was important, so was raising their family. With the high cost of daycare, it became a struggle to choose between paying for daycare or stepping out of the workforce for a few years to raise the children.

Truthfully, getting a better job is also a challenge. It can be a good long-term solution, but there is no short-term relief. Since improving your employment opportunities often requires additional education and upgrading your skills, the upfront costs of both time and money can act as a barrier for people who are already struggling to make ends meet and don't think it's a possibility at this point in their lives.

We knew we weren't alone in our struggles. With our income being near what Statistics Canada was identifying as the Canadian standard, Cam and I were truly about as average as they come when we began our debt-free journey— and in one of the more expensive regions in the country! We needed a new way to look at affordability. And today, with housing costs on the rise, now more than ever average folks like you and me need to use what we have more efficiently so that we can pay off our debt, own a home, and prepare for a comfortable retirement.

MAKE BETTER CHOICES

Cam and I began our debt-free journey by tightening our belts. We looked for ways to cut costs. We started with making choices: paying down our line of credit first, buying a home that would not only fit our budget but also allow us to meet our goals for the future, including saving enough money for our retirement. As this process developed, I realized it was more important to get the big-budget items in order first and not to worry as much about the small items. Similarly, my clients weren't always willing to cut back on their day-to-day purchases but were willing to look for efficiencies in the way they were spending their money. They viewed some of the choices they'd made as fixed decisions—things that wouldn't change, such as housing or where they were willing to live. However, these decisions were often what was causing the pain in their lives. Their big-ticket items were eating up most of the flexibility in their budget, leaving little room to save. Living this kind of lifestyle, every extra cost feels like an impossibility, with debt as the only outcome. This debt-driven lifestyle causes incredible financial stress as the debt grows over time, but these folks couldn't see any other way than what they were doing and they didn't know how to stretch the little that they had any further. This story is becoming far too common: good, hard-working people trying to make ends meet but never feeling like they are getting ahead.

If you keep going the way you are today, will you have financial security? The older I get, the more I realize that time passes much more quickly than I think it will. No one knows what's ahead, but planning today can have a huge impact on reducing future worry and stress about money. At our firm, we consistently hear one of two things from clients who are now retired: they are either grateful they came to us when they did or wish they had come to us sooner. Wouldn't it be nice to know that there is always enough money in the bank? Or that an unexpected expense or an emergency won't throw you into financial chaos? You are the only person responsible for your life, and the easiest method to approach a massive task like paying down debt or preparing for retirement is one day at a time. And you don't have to do it alone. The financial planning industry exists so that you have help in managing these major decisions. With *The Debt-Free Lifestyle* system, you take it one paycheque at a time, using cash flow that will become available once you establish a simple budget and understand your big decisions and your budget decisions.

MAKE DEBT AND SAVINGS WORK TOGETHER

Your debt, your mortgage, your retirement, and all the choices you make along the way can no longer be categorized as independent aspects of your overall financial well-being. You need to integrate them, have them work together for your greater good. If you don't unite them, you risk having a piece missing when it comes time to retire. Will you buy a home and pay a mortgage for twenty-five years only to find that you've run out of time and now have to retire "house poor" with little personal savings? Or will you opt to rent and save the difference only to find that your savings during retirement have eroded considerably because you pay an ever-increasing amount of rent and that your retirement savings are much less than you thought after you pay the tax on your registered retirement savings plan (RRSP) withdrawals?

While we were figuring out our debt-free system, Cam and I had a whole range of experiences, some good and some bad. We rented, then bought a home, had car loans, credit cards, consumer debt, and more month than money. We were not exempt from temptation and knew how easy it was to get distracted by a neighbour's new car in the driveway or the colleague who always seemed to wear the latest fashion. But the reality is that neither you nor I have any idea how much other people earn or the state of their finances. Their financial priorities might be impressing the Joneses—you! They may feel a strong need to maintain a certain appearance to their friends, their boss, or their clients to show how well they are doing. But the irony is that their financial reality could be a very different story.

I've always believed that if you're going to give advice, you need to be able to take it yourself. In my role as a financial planner, I've met with people from all walks of life, from those who are just starting out to those who have long since retired and who like to reflect on how their lives turned out. Regardless of where we are in life, it always comes down to the same truth: it's not only about how much you make but how efficiently you use what you have. I've seen clients who earn very little income be diligent with it, steward it properly, make smart decisions, and live a very comfortable, albeit modest, life. I've also met with clients who earn enough money to make you blush, but in spite of the massive amounts of income, they can't seem to stop it from rolling out the door just as quickly.

I like to think that my story is different because it's real. I've written *The Debt-Free Lifestyle* not to theorize about what may work but to show you what *is* working for my little family. This is our life, and for me, life and money are both best when they're simple. I needed a simple system that I could implement in no more than fifteen minutes every time Cam and I got paid. I also needed a system that would work for people in all stages of life who come to me for help. *The Debt-Free Lifestyle* system can put you years ahead of the game. The ultimate goal is to create freedom. When debt, including your mortgage, is no longer an issue, a world of possibilities opens up.

one

THE DEBT DILEMMA

IS DEBT HOLDING YOU BACK?

THE EVOLUTION OF DEBT

When you think back to how our grandparents lived, it was quite a different picture than what we see today. Cost of living and housing prices were lower but so were wages. People were content to buy the family home and live in it for a lifetime. Kitchens were not routinely updated to match the latest trends, and the car in the driveway had been there for the past ten years because if it was still running you didn't need a new one. Retirement at the time was funded largely by a hearty pension—the reward of a thirty-plus-year career with the same employer.

Debt was lower too. A Statistics Canada[3] report showed that in 1980 the ratio of household debt to personal disposable income was 66%, which means that for every after-tax dollar, 66 cents was needed to service a household's debt. In 2015, a high of 171% was reported by the Office of the Parliamentary Budget Officer,[4] which means that $1.71 was owed for every dollar of disposable income. Needless to say, Canadian households are overleveraged. In fact, Canadians carry the most debt-to-income of the G7 countries (which include the United States, United Kingdom, Japan, Italy, Germany, and France[5]). What is the main culprit behind the increase in this ratio? Today, people are not only carrying more consumer debt but also more debt related to housing than they ever have in the past.

IS DEBT BAD?

Some debt is good if it is used to create wealth or buy a home, increase the ability to earn income, or create a business.[6] Other debts are crimes of convenience: you want to buy a car or update your furniture or you come up against an unexpected cost. The last type of debt is not just bad but awful: consumer debt, credit cards, and high-interest loans. These debts often take advantage of those who feel like they have no other option. Everyone knows that paying 18% interest on your credit card is not wise, but here we are, doing it anyway, because we still haven't found a better way. Our lifestyle decisions are often based on taking the most that we can afford, which is why we run into trouble when things come up unexpectedly. But it's the very nature of life to be full of surprises. We need to have a game plan so that emergencies or the unexpected don't end up compromising our future.

Debt becomes bad when we overextend ourselves and lose our ability to pay back the debt, when it begins to take up so much of our disposable income that we can no longer achieve our goals. It can be downright monstrous when we get trapped in a seemingly endless cycle of payments. With the emergence of "easy credit," one of the trends that we've observed is consumers trying to fit a new monthly payment into their budget rather than getting rid of their debt as quickly as possible.[7] This approach allows the lenders to decide how much the borrower will ultimately pay, since they control the minimum payment, interest rate, and duration of the loan. Have you ever noticed that debts that are not tied to a particular asset are often left open-ended? This is the case with our credit cards and lines of credit. By not setting a defined end date, many consumers find themselves putting very little toward their principal and just continuing to give the interest away to the lenders each month.

Perhaps debt has not been vilified as much as it should be because of the role it plays in developing the economy and letting us enjoy many modern luxuries. Housing starts and the auto industry are indicators of the health of the overall economy. Both of these industries, including the jobs they create, are largely based on the consumer's ability to borrow money. In fact, major purchases by everyday people are usually made at least in part with borrowed money.[8] Borrowing means that you will owe interest, and interest is simply the premium you pay for using someone else's money. That, in and of itself, is not bad. Neither is the fact that the lender of the money will make a profit lending. If lending were not a profitable venture, the economy would not have grown as rapidly and industry would not have been able to advance at the rate that it has.[9] However, with some types of debt, the amount of interest paid can get out of hand, costing us far more than it should. Debt will always have its place, but as consumers it is our responsibility to understand it and take back control.

There is seldom a problem with debt in times of prosperity or easy credit, but the very tools that should be vehicles to create wealth can also destroy it. When the good times end, interest rates rise and the things we called assets and thought would be instrumental to our financial success can cause us stress and financial difficulty. After the 2008 market downturn, we saw how low interest rates were used to jump-start the economy and pull us out of a recession. Today, we find ourselves living with the after-effects. The past few years were a time of great opportunity for those who wanted to buy a home, or anything tied to the prime interest rate, but now we have to take a look at our personal balance sheets to ensure that our decisions are sustainable over the long run.

IS DEBT WORTH IT?

Some people like to point out that while debt has increased, so has wealth, as measured by the value of the assets we use the debt to acquire.[10] If debt was incurred obtaining assets that enhance your life, such as buying a home or starting a business, then, yes, you have most likely increased your net worth and made an investment in your future that we both hope will continue to appreciate.

However, if you are highly leveraged when interest rates rise, it may not be a question of what the asset is worth but whether your household will have sufficient means to cover the increased payment for that asset.

If this concerns you, then ask yourself the following:

- Has my budget been tailored to fit minimum payments rather than accelerated debt repayment?
- Am I maxed out now, and will this level of debt be sustainable when interest rates and payments inevitably rise? Can my budget handle that additional cost?
- Do I have a plan to become debt-free and also save for my retirement?

When we buy on credit, we often like to think that the payments we are making to have a shiny new thing are the equivalent of the sticker price. By doing so, we accept that the payments are necessary in order to have the thing we want now. However, if it is not appreciating in value, we can end up paying considerably more once the interest is factored into the price. We need to ask ourselves, Is it really worth the price we have to pay? We so often fail to look at what we're giving up in order to continue to service our debt.

There comes a point when leverage begins to work against us. We find ourselves overpaying for our purchases, which holds us back from reaching our goals and preparing for the future. We need to keep in mind that by dragging out debt repayment, even a debt with a low interest rate held for a prolonged period of time, can cost a large amount of money. So we also need to ask ourselves, Are we really taking advantage of low interest rates so that we can do other things with our money or did we just simply get lucky that rates were low because we didn't have any other options?

GETTING EDUCATED

When I went to high school, the basics of debt management were taught in only one of the three math courses offered: Consumer Finance. Unfortunately, because it was the only math class that did not count toward university requirements, many people chose not to take it. This meant that those who were serious about pursuing a degree would forgo learning the basics of personal financial management in lieu of preparing for post-secondary education. Ironically, it is during their post-secondary time that many Canadians get their first real introduction to debt. In 2015, the Canadian Federation of Students released a study showing the amount of student debt incurred, on average, to complete different levels of education. Based on information from 2010, the study showed that a college graduate would owe $14,900, while students graduating with a bachelor's or master's degree amassed a student debt of \$26,300 and \$26,600 respectively. A doctoral student would graduate with an average debt of \$41,100.[11] The total cost of acquiring a four-year undergraduate degree in 2011 was an estimated \$55,000 for the student living at home and \$84,000 for the student living away from home. The study also included a projection of the total costs for that same four-year undergraduate degree in 2030: \$102,286 for the student living at home and \$139,380 for the student living away from home.[12] This puts new graduates at a serious disadvantage because they now need to rely on a higher wage not only to face today's high cost of living but to make their loan payments on past student debt.

If student loans weren't enough to handle, the campus is also where students often get their first taste of consumer credit. Credit card companies aggressively pursue these cash-poor students based on future earnings potential, which leads us to our second problem: high consumer debt. As I mentioned earlier, this type of debt is not just bad but awful. Consumer debt is often the fuel to the fire known as "instant gratification" or is used as a costly last resort when there seems to be no other option.

CONSUMER DEBT

Let's do ourselves a favour and divide our debt into two categories: consumer debt and mortgage debt.

If we want to get a clear picture of consumer debt, let's go straight to the source. TransUnion is one of the two organizations that maintains the credit history of Canadians—the other is Equifax. Every fiscal quarter, TransUnion[13] compiles a report segmented by province that shows the average amount of consumer debt that Canadians have, excluding their mortgages. In the fourth quarter of 2015, the Canadian average debt was $21,512, which varies by region. This type of debt broke down as follows:

TYPE	AVERAGE BALANCE BY PRODUCT
Car loans	$ 19,777
Credit cards	$ 3,810
Installment loans	$ 22,476
Lines of credit	$ 29,017

Keep in mind that different people will have a different mix of products and will not necessarily carry all or the maximum of any one type. TransUnion also tracks and reports on consumer debts that have been past due for over ninety days. Those delinquencies across Canada were 2.67% in the fourth quarter of 2015. Lower delinquency rates are good, and they show that the low interest rates that we have enjoyed make it easier for us to make our payments on certain types of debt.

To help round out the consumer debt picture, the Bank of Montreal (BMO) also releases an annual debt report.[14] In 2014, BMO found that based on their survey results, 52% of

Canadians owe money on their credit cards, 43% have mortgages, and 15% have student loans. Perhaps the most alarming part was that by 2015 debt had increased and 46% of those with debt plan to take on more in the coming year.

So even though interest rates have been low, we still need access to debt. These are the good days and yet reduced interest rates and lower mortgage payments haven't kept us out of consumer debt, even though these low rates should be freeing up cash flow that we can use elsewhere. Why, then, do we have this consumer debt? Is it because we're all terribly reckless spenders who are unaware of the consequences of our actions? I don't believe that's the case. I think that given the choice, those who have debt would rather not have it but have found themselves in that position from unexpected expenses or because they didn't have a method of organizing their finances in the first place. Perhaps the bigger question is, What will happen when the tables turn and interest rates increase, when it will cost us more to service our debts?

ARE LOW INTEREST RATES WORRY-FREE?

The 2015 BMO Annual Debt Report also indicated that an interest rate increase of only 2% would cause 64% of Canadian households with debt to feel stressed about their finances. These reported feelings of potential financial stress were higher in provinces with higher costs of living. In British Columbia, that number was 71% and in Ontario it was 69%. The unnerving part is that a 2% increase in interest rates doesn't sound like very much, especially with interest rates currently at historic lows.

What's the big deal about interest rates? Why would a small increase cause so much stress, and should we be getting worried too? Let's break down our debt further to see what an increase would actually mean.

Interest is the premium you pay to a lender for the use of its money. Essentially, interest is the cost of borrowing and is often expressed as a percentage of the loan. This tells us a few things: If the loan is open-ended, we won't know how much our total interest cost will be until the loan is paid off. If we take more time to pay it off, it will cost us more money, as we'll continue to pay out that interest for a longer period of time. If the interest rate becomes higher, or is high to begin with, it will cost us more money. So while the loan may cost you more in the long run if interest rates increase, interest rates affect both the lifetime cost of the loan and the length of time it can take you to pay off the loan.

Credit cards are a great example. If you're able to pay off your balance every month, credit cards can be incredibly convenient. They can be used for larger purchases without question, as you're already prequalified for the credit limit on the card. They can also make online shopping possible and some types of payments much easier. But for all those conveniences, credit card interest rates are excruciatingly high.

Since we know that the interest is essentially our cost of borrowing, let's look at the other side of the equation: the principal.

Think of the principal as the amount you initially borrowed. While the credit card companies can choose between different ways to calculate the blend of principal and interest in your payment, the minimum payment is usually a set dollar amount or a percentage of your balance outstanding. This percentage can be as low as 2%, 3%, or 4% but will vary based on the terms of each different card. If your interest rate is 18% and you never make more than the minimum payment, you can literally spend decades and thousands of dollars in interest before fully discharging your debt, depending on the size of your outstanding balance.[15] Talk about an expensive purchase!

Consumer debt is still a relatively small part of Canadians' total debt picture, but since the interest rates can be the highest in this segment, it can't be ignored. Your best bet is to pay off your debts with the highest interest rates first, and then focus on the debts with lower interest rates. When you can, consolidate debts onto a line of credit or into your mortgage to get a lower rate. This can decrease your total costs for that debt and may even help shorten the length of time that you have it outstanding. If you do so, you need to make sure you increase the payments you make to correspond with the amount you've increased the line of credit or mortgage.

WHAT HAPPENS WHEN INTEREST RATES INCREASE?

Here's how an increase in interest rates can affect different types of debt:

CREDIT CARDS: Some debts like credit cards have interest rates that are already so high they will remain unaffected. This isn't something to be happy about; it means that if you're carrying a balance, you're already overpaying.

DEBTS WITH VARIABLE INTEREST RATES: These types of loans will feel the impact of interest rate increases immediately. From lines of credit to certain types of mortgages, the amount of interest that needs to be paid will go up instantly with a rate increase, which will increase total costs and can increase the length of time to pay off the debt.

DEBTS WITH FIXED INTEREST RATES: These debts can range from a car loan to a mortgage and last for a specified amount of time. For debts with fixed terms, there will be a delay, which could be months or years, between the time the interest rate changes and the time the term comes up for renewal.

Debts with fixed or variable interest rates are often calculated as prime plus a certain percentage, based on each individual's credit rating.[16] Because the mortgage takes up a large percentage of our budget, an increase here can make a real difference in the amount we have left to spend on other things.

MORTGAGE DEBT

After a year of renting a condo in British Columbia, Cam and I, like many others, found out that with interest rates so low we could buy a home. In our opinion, few things are more satisfying than having a place that is truly our own. As most do, we went through the traditional process of finding out how much of a mortgage we could qualify for and began shopping around. We were living in Abbotsford, but with my new job in New Westminster, commuting would take well over an hour. Since Cam was working in Langley, we decided to find a place in the middle to even out our commute times. We settled on Surrey, choosing a townhouse primarily because it was the most square footage we could get for our dollar at the time.

Over these past few years, low interest rates have been a catalyst for multitudes of eager first-time buyers, and developers have been on trend. In the Canada Mortgage and Housing Corporation (CMHC)'s fourth-quarter 2015 Housing Market Outlook, housing starts were projected to range between 153,000 and 203,000 new units in 2016 and between 149,000 and 199,000 new units in 2017. Those are new builds, but existing houses are changing hands as well, with the Multiple Listings Services® (MLS®) sales expected to be between 425,000 and 534,000 units in 2016 and between 416,000 and 536,000 units in 2017.[17] That's a lot of houses—and a lot of mortgages.

HOW DOES A MORTGAGE WORK?

If you've taken on, or are about to take on, one of the biggest financial obligations of your life, you should spend some time understanding how your mortgage works. There are two parts to every mortgage payment you make: the principal repayment, which builds your equity, and the interest cost, which is the premium you pay the lender to borrow its money in the first place. This point is really important because you can save yourself a ton of time and money by being aware of this blend in your repayment schedule.

The Financial Consumer Agency of Canada has some great resources about mortgages[18] and home ownership, as does CMHC,[19] Canada's national housing agency. When you talk to a lender or your mortgage broker, you'll start to hear a liberal amount of industry jargon, so let's begin by defining some of the most important terms.

AMORTIZATION PERIOD: It helps to think of the amortization period as the lifespan of your mortgage. The typical mortgage lifespan is currently twenty-five years. The maximum length of this lifespan can be influenced by legislation and by the organization making the loan.[20] It can also be influenced by your decisions. In Canada, mortgages are most commonly partially amortized.[21] This means that every time the term comes up for renewal, the other details of the loan can also be negotiated. You can shorten your amortization period by making prepayments on your mortgage or change it by refinancing. Anytime there is a change to the amortization schedule, it will also affect the total cost of your mortgage.

In contrast, in the United States, mortgages are more commonly fully amortized, meaning everything gets locked in when the deal is initially signed. The good part is that this ensures the mortgage will be fully paid off by the time it expires. Partial amortization is more flexible, but it can get quite expensive for the borrower if he or she chooses to move backward on the amortization schedule by lengthening the mortgage after refinancing or after a rate increase to make the payments more affordable. Just like we saw with credit cards, this can result in the borrower grossly overpaying for the original purchase.

TERM: The term is the length of time that you agree to certain conditions, including the interest rate and payment amount. According to the Bank of Canada, over 95% of mortgages have a term of five years or less.[22] If you choose a fixed rate for those five years, you know what the payment will be. Once the term is expired, if you still have an outstanding balance, you will negotiate another term with your lender and at that point your mortgage payment will change.

PRINCIPAL: Your principal is the amount that you borrowed from your lender. As you pay off more of your principal, that portion of the house becomes "yours." That paid-off portion is what we then call your equity.

INTEREST: The amount of interest you will pay is expressed as a percentage, calculated on the outstanding mortgage balance. That percentage is called the interest rate. Pay close attention to how frequently the interest is compounded. More frequent compounding can increase your cost.

FIXED RATE: A fixed rate will stay the same for the length of your term. This means that you will know what your payments will be for that period of time.

VARIABLE RATE: A variable rate can change at any time. It is usually tied to the prime rate, plus a certain percentage depending on the type of credit risk you are categorized as being.

OPEN MORTGAGE: You can prepay as much as you want, whenever you want.

CLOSED MORTGAGE: A closed mortgage means that you cannot make any additional payments unless you have a specified prepayment privilege. While it is common for these types of mortgages to have prepayment privileges, there can be significant penalties if you exceed them.

PREPAYMENT PRIVILEGES: This is the ability to put extra money down toward your principal. Most closed mortgages will express this as a percentage of your original mortgage balance, such as 10% to 20%. If you plan to make prepayments, you should also ask your lender for the dollar amount each year so that you don't overpay and face a penalty.

PREPAYMENT PENALTIES: In some instances, if you want to make a prepayment in excess of your prepayment privilege, or pay off the whole mortgage early, you may be able to do it under the provisions of the Federal Interest Act, but you will be penalized. The calculation done is known as the interest rate differential (IRD)and you'll want to have your lender do it for you. Commonly, your charge will be the greater of three months' interest or the difference between the current interest rate and your interest rate for the time you have remaining on your term.[23] Some closed mortgages may not allow prepayments at all, so be sure to check with your lender or review your contract before you prepay.

PREPAYMENT RISK: Let's reverse the situation for a minute so that you're sitting on the other side of the desk, in the lender's shoes. His or her employer, the bank or mortgage company, doesn't want you to prepay your mortgage. In fact, it doesn't want you to do it so badly that it's given it a name and tasked its actuaries with working out what it will do to its profits if you do. Remember the amount of interest that you've been paying out on a regular basis? Banks are known for consistent earnings, and a lot of that consistency comes from the fact that we're giving them large amounts of interest over a long period of time. That's why the option to prepay, or having an open mortgage, may cause you to have a higher interest rate. If the lenders feel that they have to risk you putting extra money down and disrupting their cash flow from the mortgage, then they will charge you extra.

WHAT IS THE AVERAGE MORTGAGE DEBT?

For our purposes, we should divide our borrowers into two types: those who have just bought a home and are fully leveraged and those who are well into their mortgage. The people in the second group may have reduced their debt enough to create a buffer against rising interest rates in the coming years. Interest on the mortgage is calculated on the outstanding balance, so rising interest rates will have less of an impact on a lower mortgage amount than a higher one when a term comes up for renewal. While the higher interest rate can mean that the payment will go up, a lower balance can offset some of that increase, depending on the amount of the increase and the amount of the outstanding balance.

According to the spring 2015 Manulife Bank of Canada Homeowner Debt Survey and Manulife Bank's Debt Research,[24] the average mortgage debt in Canada is $190,000. This varies across the provinces, with Alberta registering the highest average mortgage debt of $242,400 and British Columbia in a close second at $217,600. This means that with a mortgage balance of $200,000, Cam and I fit the profile of the average Canadian who is well into the process. While we now have an idea of the average mortgage debt carried by Canadians, what about new buyers? What is the average cost of buying a home? Through a number of resources such as the Multiple Listing Service® (MLS®), the Canadian Real Estate Association (CREA) can map and track housing sales trends across Canada, complete with volumes and prices. This means that it can tell us the national average of housing prices across the country and by region. In May 2015, the national average price of a home was $450,008. By January 2016, Vancouver was listed as the most expensive city, with an average home price of $1,083,177.[25] In Toronto, it was $631,092. Living in a major city can have a much larger price tag, and the Toronto Real Estate Board reported in January 2016 that the average price for a detached home in Toronto's 416 area code was $1,061,789.[26]

MEET OUR HAPPY FAMILIES

In addition to our real-life example, two fictitious couples based on two key demographics are helping to round out *The Debt-Free Lifestyle* system.

MOM & POP AVERAGE: Mom & Pop Average are a nice, friendly couple in their forties who live in Winnipeg. They met in their early thirties, got married, and had three kids. They rented and saved their money until they could afford to buy. They put 5% down on a house near the national average price. This qualified them for a mortgage, but because they didn't have the full 20% to put down, they were required to add on mortgage loan insurance. They ended up with a mortgage outstanding of $450,000. Since the kids are still young, Mom & Pop Average plan on staying in this home for a good number of years but are a bit concerned since they have only begun to pay for their mortgage at this stage in life. They figure they will need to work well into their sixties just to continue making their mortgage payments. While they've been faithfully putting money into registered education savings plans (RESPs) for the kids, they've got little savings of their own due to the cost of raising a family. They are wondering how they will find the money to take care of everything all at once.

MR. METRO: Mr. Metro is in his fifties. He is divorced and has one son, now in his twenties, from his marriage. Junior is just finishing off university, and due to the high cost of living in their city, he decided to stay at home while completing his studies. But now in his last year, job prospects are bleak and he thinks he may have to stay home for a few more years until he can get on his feet. Mr. Metro and Junior live in a detached house in Toronto Central, which is very convenient but expensive. In addition, after making payments on the family home for years, Mr. Metro had to pay the former Mrs. Metro a hefty sum to retain the family home, which meant he needed to refinance. Mr. Metro can't believe that at his age, he isn't further ahead. He has a great job in management for a large national company and makes a generous salary. He has a pension plan at work and has been contributing to his registered retirement savings plan (RRSP) for years. However, his divorce was lengthy and his cash flow has been strained by the need to pay spousal support. The RESP for Junior ran out last year, and he wants his son to begin life without debt, so he has been footing the bill. Due to all of the demands on his money, he ran up a large credit card bill and had to refinance for the second time just to get some relief. His solution to his cash flow problems has always been to work harder, but now he is feeling like he's running out of time. While his home is valued at $1,500,000, he still owes $1,000,000, which is just under the average price of a detached home in the city of Toronto.[27] He is beginning to wonder when he can afford to stop working, since he still needs to pay down a substantial amount on his mortgage.

CAM & I: We were married in our early twenties and moved to British Columbia in our mid-twenties, buying our town-house in Surrey a year after we arrived. With our modest salaries, we learned the importance of having a good handle on where our money was going on a weekly basis, which has been the foundation of our success. We have contributed regularly to our RRSPs throughout the whole process but needed to figure out the best use of the remainder of the free cash flow that our budgeting created. We are both strongly averse to debt, and so this preference put debt freedom as our main goal. We knew that since we started so young, we would have a large amount of time that we could save money once the mortgage obligation was out of the way. But should

Mom & Pop Average and Mr. Metro look at their situations the same way?

Our three families represent different stages in life and difference circumstances. Cam & I are in our thirties, and our real-life example represents both new homebuyers and the couple who is already well into their mortgage with a mortgage balance of $200,000. Mom & Pop Average are in their forties with a young, growing family and bought a home priced near the national average. Mr. Metro is in his fifties, divorced and supporting his university-aged son and also has the costs associated with owning a home in a metropolitan area. We've all made different big decisions based on our family size, income level, and where it was important for us to live. We've purchased homes that range in value quite dramatically. Yet we're all faced with the same questions: Should we save money or focus on paying down our mortgage? What are the long-term effects of our lifestyle choices? Will our decisions ultimately lead us to a secure and stress-free retirement?

LOCATION, LOCATION, LOCATION

Where you choose to live will play a role in determining how much of a house you can afford in more ways than you may think. First, housing costs vary widely by province and by city. Second, when lenders calculate how much you can afford, they take into account things like property tax and heating costs, which can also vary widely by region. This means that you might qualify for a larger mortgage in a city with lower property taxes and heating costs than you would in a city with higher costs.

Let's take a look at how the different places where we choose to live and the housing values affect the amount of mortgage that we can qualify for.

Cam & I live in Surrey, where the residential property tax rate[28] on our home valued at $275,000 is $1,307 a year, or $109 a month. Estimated heating costs[29] are $550 for the year, or $46 a month. We also had a maintenance fee for our townhouse that started out at $267 a month.

Mom & Pop Average live in Winnipeg. They needed a big home and found one in a desirable neighbourhood. They purchased a home for $450,000, but after their down payment and mortgage loan insurance were factored in and closing costs were paid, the mortgage balance was still $450,000. In Winnipeg, the property taxes for a house that price are an approximate $5,131 a year,[30] or $428 a month, and heating costs are an average of $1,776 a year, [31] or $148 a month.

Mr. Metro lives in Toronto, where the current residential property tax rate for a home valued at $1,500,000[32] is $10,584 a year,[33] or $882 a month. We'll estimate the heating costs at $1,082 a year, or $90 a month. He has had this mortgage for a number of years already, but due to refinancing twice his current balance outstanding on the mortgage is $1,000,000.

When applicable, municipal homeowner grants were factored in.

UNDERSTANDING DEBT SERVICE RATIOS

When lenders reach for their calculators to determine how much a family can afford to take on as a mortgage, they will factor in a few different things, one of which is your debt service ratio.

Debt service ratios determine how much of your family income you can commit to housing costs, based on lending guidelines. Currently through CMHC, the gross debt service ratio (GDSR) is 35% of gross family income and the total debt service ratio (TDSR) is 42%.[34] This means that the housing costs detailed in this ratio shouldn't exceed 35% of the gross family income and the housing costs plus the cost to service other debts should not exceed 42%. The ratios used can change based on the lender, and what follows may vary from what a lender would actually offer. Lenders can actually offer more to people with good credit and low or no debt.[35] Lenders will also do a calculation called the loan-to-value ratio, which determines what percentage of the assessed property value will be financed, and this metric is based on your down payment. We will take a closer look at the loan-to-value ratio later. The lenders will use the lower of the two to ensure that the property you buy is one that you can afford.[36] While CMHC's lending rates are used in these examples, other companies may offer a higher ratio. For example, lenders may currently loan up to 44% of gross income for people with good credit.[37] The calculations for our happy couples were done using both GDSR and TDSR, assumes that each family has a cost to service their debts of $100 per month, and doesn't factor in the effect of the downpayment on affordability.

UNDERSTANDING INTEREST RATES AND THE LENDING RATIOS

One of the other key factors in determining how much of a house we can actually afford is the interest rate. Note that there are two different factors at play here: the first is the assessed value of the property, which determines the property taxes, and the second is the mortgage amount that each individual family will need to support. The following chart compares what the mortgages would cost our happy families each month with a 4% interest rate.

			HOUSEHOLD INCOME	
	MORTGAGE BALANCE	MORTGAGE PAYMENT (4%)	GDSR	TDSR
Cam & I	$ 200,000	$ 1,052	$ 45,954	$ 41,152
Mom & Pop Average	$ 450,000	$ 2,367	$ 100,890	$ 86,932
Mr. Metro	$ 1,000,000	$ 5,260	$ 213,681	$ 180,925

The columns to the right show what the income of each of the three families would have to be based on the debt service criteria. This would all be great if interest rates stayed static or didn't move around too much, but with mortgages, we are dealing with twenty-five-year periods of time. A lot can happen in twenty-five years.

WHAT HAPPENS WHEN INTEREST RATES GO UP?

According to Genworth Canada,[38] in 1995 the average prime rate was 8.5% and the average Canadian family income was $54,583. At the time this worked because housing prices, and as a result mortgage balances, were much lower than they are today. In 2014, the average prime rate was 2.89% and the Canadian average family income was $74,540. Now mortgages are usually prime plus a certain amount, depending on your credit rating and other factors.

Let's look at our three families again. Assuming that the interest rate on each of their mortgages is 8%, how does that 8% affect the amount of income they need to stay within these constraints?

	MORTGAGE BALANCE	MORTGAGE PAYMENT (8%)	HOUSEHOLD INCOME	
			GDSR	TDSR
Cam & I	$ 200,000	$ 1,526	$ 62,219	$ 54,706
Mom & Pop Average	$ 450,000	$ 3,434	$ 137,486	$ 117,429
Mr. Metro	$ 1,000,000	$ 7,632	$ 295,005	$ 248,694

The columns to the right show the amount of family income each household would need to qualify for a mortgage of that amount using CMHC's current debt service ratios. According to the chart on page 37, Mom & Pop Average could get their $450,000 house at 4% with a household income of $100,890 using the GDSR once the costs of living in their region were factored in. But if rates were 8%, instead of 4% at the time of purchase, they would need a family income of $137,486 to get into the exact same mortgage. Perhaps the bigger challenge is that the payment would be over $1,000 per month higher. The TDSR shows what they could qualify with if they have other debt. The TDSR may be higher or lower than the GDSR depending on the amount of debt showing on each family's credit bureau report.

Mr. Metro finds himself in an even more dire situation because his mortgage is much larger. With his $ 1,000,000 mortgage, the larger outstanding balance on the mortgage serves to amplify the effects of the interest rate.

Now, this is a concern because we want to ensure that the home we qualify for today is still affordable tomorrow. To give you an idea of how big of a role the interest rate plays into affordability in terms of our monthly payments, here is a look at all three families' mortgage amounts and what the monthly payment would cost if the initial amount were taken out at different interest rates. This rates are based on the mortgage lasting for twenty-five years.

	INTEREST RATE[39]					
	4%	6%	8%	10%	12%	14%
$ 200,000	$ 1,052	$ 1,280	$ 1,526	$ 1,789	$ 2,064	$ 2,348
$ 450,000	$ 2,367	$ 2,879	$ 3,434	$ 4,025	$ 4,644	$ 5,282
$ 1,000,000	$ 5,260	$ 6,398	$ 7,632	$ 8,945	$ 10,319	$ 11,739

HOW DO LOW INTEREST RATES HELP?

Low interest rates do help people get into homes for the first time or buy the bigger home that they've been dreaming of. Refinancing when interest rates are low is also widely used to pay less interest on consumer debt. Perhaps the best part of lower rates is that they benefit everyone with an existing mortgage whose term comes up for renewal during that time period. This is because, by the very nature of low interest rates, more money from each payment automatically gets attributed to the principal repayment. So without doing a thing, you're getting ahead. In fact, it extends beyond home-owners. A continued low interest rate environment is hugely beneficial to anyone looking to pay down their debts quickly, as long as those debts are tied to the prime rate.

CAN WE AFFORD INCREASING PAYMENTS?

If it comes time to renew an existing mortgage and interest rates are lower, we will find that our monthly payment has gone down to adjust for the lower interest rate. Most of us will just take that extra money and spend it in other places. While it's true that this is good for the overall economy, we also need to think about how it affects our personal fiscal well-being.

That's because, unfortunately, this works both ways: when rates increase and the term comes up for renewal, there may be less to spend due to a higher mortgage payment. Those same folks may find themselves needing to extend the length of their mortgage to keep their payments manageable and able to fit into their monthly budget. However, that type of action is not really a solution since the extra time you will spend paying into your mortgage means that you will pay more interest and have a higher cost than you had anticipated when you originally signed up. In this scenario, compound interest is working against you. Like we saw in the previous example, the bigger the mortgage, the bigger the problem.

Now wait a second, you may say. If I have qualified for a mortgage, wouldn't the lender have already anticipated a higher interest rate scenario? By virtue of them giving me the money, shouldn't I be okay?

Lenders do have a way of determining whether you can handle higher payments. It's called stress testing, and it is required by the Office of the Superintendent of Financial Institutions (OSFI) that any federally regulated financial institution has the means of testing its mortgage portfolios.[40] Provincially regulated lenders have similar requirements in place. If you choose a variable rate, or a term that is less than five years, your lender needs to look at the current rate of a five-year fixed rate term and ensure that your debt service ratios can handle that.[41] In addition, the Minister of Justice releases eligible mortgage loan regulations that must be followed.[42] The actual process of stress testing for further rate increases may vary by lender and some will show more diligence than others. Will rising interest rates affect you? It will all depend on how your mortgage is structured, when and how quickly interest rates go up, and the balance outstanding that you have when they do.

One more question, you say. If I'm paying my mortgage down every month, won't that compensate for potential interest rate increases?

It may. For example, let's take another look at Mom & Pop Average's mortgage. This $450,000 mortgage has a lifespan of twenty-five years and five-year terms. The twenty-five years, called the amortization period, is really just the lifetime of the mortgage—how long it is designed to last. If within that twenty-five-year period Mom & Pop Average choose five-year fixed rate terms, that means there will be five opportunities for the amount of their payment to change over the lifetime of the mortgage.

IF HISTORY REVERSED ITSELF

As an overall trend, interest rates have been on the decline for the past twenty-five years, with some ups and downs along the way.[43] This has made it an incredibly good time for homeowners, as not only are they paying down their mortgages but on average future renewals also just keep getting less expensive. As the old saying goes, though, what goes up must come down. Let's now look at the Bank of Canada's published average residential five-year mortgage lending rate[44] and reverse it so we find ourselves on the other side of mortgage rate history.

Using the Bank of Canada list, let's take the interest rate on January 1 for each of the five-year periods from 1995 to 2015 and playback the past twenty-five years in reverse.

Let's begin with Mom & Pop Average's $450,000 mortgage.

	INTEREST RATE	PAYMENT	CUMULATIVE DIFFERENCE	BALANCE END TERM	CUMULATIVE INTEREST
Years 1–5	3.96%	$ 2,357.34	$ 0.00	$ 391,469	$ 82,910
Years 6–10	4.80%	$ 2,530.34	$ 173.00	$ 325,249	$ 168,510
Years 11–15	5.60%	$ 2,663.73	$ 306.39	$ 245,046	$ 248,131
Years 16–20	8.34%	$ 2,998.87	$ 641.53	$ 147,209	$ 330,226
Years 21–25	10.60%	$ 3,154.86	$ 797.52	$ 0	$ 372,308

This shows that even though they are paying down the mortgage, payments (as shown in the "Difference" column) can still increase due to a higher interest rate.

Now consider Mr. Metro's $1,000,000 mortgage.

Let's see what would happen to Mr. Metro's larger mortgage payments if he held the $1,000,000 mortgage through this period of time, using all the same assumptions as before.

	INTEREST RATE	PAYMENT	CUMULATIVE DIFFERENCE	BALANCE END TERM	CUMULATIVE INTEREST
Years 1–5	3.96%	$ 5,238.54	$ 0.00	$ 869,932	$ 184,244
Years 6–10	4.80%	$ 5,622.99	$ 384.45	$ 722,775	$ 374,467
Years 11–15	5.60%	$ 5,919.40	$ 680.86	$ 544,545	$ 551,401
Years 16–20	8.34%	$ 6,664.14	$ 1,425.60	$ 327,129	$ 733,833
Years 21–25	10.60%	$ 7,010.75	$ 1,772.21	$ 0	$ 827,349

With these increases, the payment ended up being $1,772.21 a month, or $21,266.52 a year more than when the mortgage began. That represents 11% of Mr. Metro's original gross qualifying income. Why does Mr. Metro's mortgage see so much more of an increase than Mom & Pop Average's? The balance at the end of each term remains high since his original balance was high to begin with, so the effects of the increased rates are felt on each dollar that remains on his mortgage. If Mr. Metro found himself leveraged to the max, finding the extra money to pay for his increased mortgage payments may be a huge strain. This will not only compromise Mr. Metro's ability to save, but he may also have to refinance and re-extend the amortization period to keep his payment manageable. If rates continued to increase, he would end up paying more than expected for his mortgage and would have wasted a lot of good money just playing catch-up.

UNDERSTANDING YOUR PAYMENTS

As mentioned, your mortgage payment includes two parts: the principal repayment, which builds equity, and the interest portion, which is paid directly to the lender. In an amortization schedule, your payment is a blend of the two, and for the first half of the mortgage more interest is paid than principal. The Financial Consumer Agency of Canada says it best:

> *At first, most of your payments go towards the interest. In the first years of the mortgage, the principal, or the amount*

that you owe, may decrease by only a small amount. As the mortgage balance decreases over time, more of your payment is used to pay off the principal.[45]

Think of your interest payment as a sunk cost. You will need to pay it regardless, but once it's paid, every additional dollar goes toward reducing principal. When interest rates are low, not only will your mortgage cost less, but there is less of a hurdle to jump over before you begin putting more of the money toward your principal.

On the other hand, if your mortgage term comes up after an interest rate increase, and the payment feels unmanageable, the lender may suggest that you extend the length of the mortgage so that the monthly payment becomes easier to handle. While this may feel like a win in the short-term, it is the kind of decision that will cost you major dollars in the long-term.

UNDERSTANDING OPPORTUNITY COST

Have you ever had the nagging feeling that the weight of your debt is keeping you from pursuing other opportunities? A concept called "opportunity cost" is often used in business to weigh two alternative courses of action against each other. You can use it for yourself by asking, Out of the two paths I can choose, which will get me further ahead and by how much? The question then becomes, How much will I not only gain from choosing one option over the other but also lose if I choose the competing course of action?

Think of it in terms of your debt. Missed opportunities and poor structure do have a cost associated with them, especially when you keep in mind that we all have a limited amount of time to acquire money before we stop working. The amount that we are able to save will have a direct impact on our standard of living during retirement. So regardless of where we are in our lives, we need to ask ourselves if we're making the best possible decisions while there's still time. Are we maximizing our resources and ultimately making choices that work together cohesively to lead us toward a comfortable retirement?

The two areas of concern in a rising interest rate environment are affordability and opportunity cost. To determine the best use of your money, you need to look at your total cost paid into the mortgage over its lifetime, at the current interest rate, with some allowance for rate increases. This information can provide you with what you'll need to determine the opportunity cost of different courses of action.

Let's look at Mom & Pop Average's $450,000 mortgage in three different scenarios and compare the costs. The first will show low interest rates that increase slightly after the first fifteen years. The second will show a 2% increase with every five-year term, and the third will show a higher rate that decreases slightly. We will use an amortization period of twenty-five years and have chosen five-year terms.

INTEREST RATES	TOTAL PAYMENTS	TOTAL CUMULATIVE INTEREST
Low: 4% for first 15 years, 6% for next 10 years	$ 736,997	$ 286,997
Rising: 2% increase per term Starting at 4%, ending at 12%	$ 918,137	$ 468,137
High, slight decrease: 14% for first 15 years, 12% for next 10 years	$ 1,538,652	$ 1,088,652

Can you see how paying down a mortgage in different interest rate environments can have considerable impact on your total payments? For that same $450,000 home, the interest rate plays a significant role in how much cumulative interest you will pay over the lifetime of your mortgage and also how much money will come out of your pocket to pay for the house overall. Now, the interest rate is something that is outside of our control. So we need to find something that is within our control to be able to manage.

Have you ever wondered why a mortgage lasts twenty-five years? Over a twenty-five-year period if interest rates remain high, you can end up paying far more than the value of your home in interest payments.

Stop and think about that for a minute.

In our high interest rate scenario, during the lifetime of the mortgage, the total payments were over three times the amount of the mortgage. If that were your home, do you think that's a good use of your money? Is your home worth three times the price that you bought it for, especially since property values are already so high? Can you think of better things that you could do with that money, such as a guilt-free vacation or making sure you have enough money to retire comfortably? Your house alone could hold the secret not only to your debt freedom but also to ensuring that you have the ability to save for the future.

DEBT AND RETIREMENT: THE ULTIMATE OPPORTUNITY

Twice a year, Manulife Bank conducts a Homeowner Debt Survey,[46] and in spring 2015, it found that debt freedom was a high priority for 78% of the respondents. Of those surveyed, 56% had reduced their debt in the past year, and if they found themselves debt-free tomorrow, 71% would direct at least some of the extra money into retirement savings.

You see, there are two major parts to your finances: the part you have to live with today and the part you'll have to live with in the future. In your retirement, you will no longer be earning an income and your level of comfort will be based on the income you receive from government benefits, your pension plan (if you are lucky enough to have one), and your personal savings. Barring any type of inheritance, this is it. Your actions today play a big role in the quality of your golden years. Your current choices around your debt, your budget, and your big decisions will have a ripple effect across your life and determine your future.

Even if retirement is the furthest thing from your mind today, many Canadians are looking for ways to get ahead, and with a growing propensity toward debt freedom. But a low national savings rate of around 4%[47] seems to show that life keeps getting in the way. In the Homeowner Debt Survey, when mortgage holders were asked why they didn't put any additional money toward their mortgage in the past year, the biggest reason for 61% of respondents was that they didn't have extra money, other spending priorities accounted for 22%, and 16% of respondents did make additional payments toward other debts. Interestingly, only 13% said that they didn't make extra payments on their mortgage because of a low interest rate.

When we start to look at why people don't feel they have extra money, we need to look at how much of a person's income is going toward housing and servicing their existing debts and how much remains to go toward their lifestyle. According to the CPA Household Finances in Canada report,[48] the most recent data set (2013) showed that 8.8% of disposable income for a family living in British Columbia is going toward servicing the interest portion of their total debt. In Ontario the percentage of this debt-service ratio was 7.5%, and in Manitoba it was 6.2%. Nationally, the Canadian average is 7.1% of disposable income going toward servicing the interest portion of their debt. That is a lot of the average person's income.

If we can find a way to wipe out our consumer and mortgage debt quickly, then we can turn around and apply this new cash flow toward securing our financial future. Your debt is a sure thing. It's not going to go away unless you work at it. Let's start with a simple method of managing your money so that you can determine where the money will come from to begin with.

two

THE SIMPLE BUDGET

YOUR KEY TO BEING DEBT-FREE

Budgeting. Even the word leaves a bitter taste in most people's mouths. When you mention it, people divide into two camps: those who can't be bothered and will avoid it at all costs (bills pile up on the corner of the dining room table, ignored until the end of the month) and those who take it to the other extreme. They have spreadsheets for everything; every transaction has been documented, every spending pattern is mapped, organized by colour, and archived. For the sheer amount of time this exercise involves, these people find themselves in the minority.

It takes a certain type of personality to be able to stick with a complicated budget, month in, month out, for years on end. The majority of us, myself included, won't continue with a process that is time-consuming or complex on a long-term basis, so my budgeting system is fast and easy. Once you know your monthly expenses, it shouldn't take any more than fifteen minutes every time you get paid to budget, and because it's so quick, it's much more likely that you'll stick with it. However, the best part about having a budget is that it puts you in control. You know where your money is going every week, and you can make decisions and set priorities based on what is important to you.

THE SIMPLE BUDGET SYSTEM

We all have a limited amount of income to spend, so we need to ensure that we're maximizing the use of each dollar. In order to be successful, we need to create a certain amount of free cash flow, which is an amount of money we can use to accelerate our debt repayment or other financial goals each month. First, look at your paystub to find out your net amount, which is your take-home pay—the amount deposited into your bank account after deductions and tax withholding. Here is what our income looked like when we began: my monthly net income was $2,400, while Cam's monthly net income was $2,200.

Next, create a list ordered by the date of every expense withdrawn from your bank account. This list includes only mandatory expenses, which are the bills you need to pay to keep the lights on and a roof over your head. At this point, don't list expenses that can change each period.

Here's what our month looked like:

DAY OF THE MONTH	EXPENSE	DOLLAR AMOUNT
2	Critical Illness Insurance	$ 6.00
2	ICBC Van Insurance	$ 250.00
3	ICBC Car Insurance	$ 125.00
4	Monthly bank fee	$ 14.95
5	Maintenance fee	$ 267.00
5	Fortis Natural Gas	$ 46.00
10	Critical Illness Insurance	$ 26.00
12	Cell Phone	$ 100.80
18	Life Insurance	$ 25.00
19	Disability Insurance	$ 87.00
19	Netflix	$ 8.00
21	BC Medical	$ 96.00
25	TV/phone/internet	$ 230.00
28	Life Insurance	$ 44.00
28	RRSP deposit	$ 50.00
28	RRSP deposit	$ 50.00
30	Bus Pass	$ 99.00
TOTAL		**$ 1,524.75**

Variable:	Food	$ 600.00 a month/$ 150.00 a week
	Fuel	$ 400.00 a month/$ 100.00 a week
Bi-monthly:	BC Hydro	$ 102.00 on average bi-monthly
Annual:	Water	$ 408.00 on average per year
	Contents insurance	$ 420.00 on average per year

You'll notice right away that I didn't include a line for our mortgage, which we chose for the incredible flexibility around the amount of payment we apply toward the house every month. More on that later. Each time a paycheque is deposited into our account, we figure out how much will go toward the bills in that period. It's really great if you and your partner get paid on alternating weeks because then you only need to budget for a week at a time. We are then able to decide how much we have available to spend that week and how much remains to go toward our financial goals.

So, if last Thursday was the first of the month and Cam got paid, $1,100 was deposited into the account. I would add up the expenses using the dates on my chart from the 1st to my paycheque on the 8th. For that time period, we'd need to ensure that $709 remains in the account, untouched, to pay the bills we know are coming in.

We also know that we'll spend about $150 that week in groceries/miscellaneous items and $100 for fuel, so we need to keep a total of $959 available for the week. I'm not so concerned with tracking every dollar spent on groceries/miscellaneous or gas, as long as it comes in at or under the amount I've budgeted. If you're concerned that you'll overspend, pull out the money in cash, and don't spend more than you have until the next pay period. We also like to keep a $500 float in the account in case any surprises come up before we get paid again.

In my example, there wouldn't be much left over that first week. But the following week, with my $1,200 paycheque, our expenses, including food and fuel, would total only $377. I know I have $823 that can go toward debt repayment that week, and in our case, that means our mortgage. I run these numbers every week, the day we each get paid. Then I subtract my variable expenses, such as entertainment or clothing costs for that pay period, and transfer the remaining money immediately out of the account and put it toward our debt. Once you've been doing it for a while, it takes about fifteen minutes.

Once you've completed your budget and have a list of all of your mandatory bills, everything else falls into the category of discretionary spending. This is where it's different for every family. For the first time, you may be seeing that you should have a lot of money available, but you feel like you don't. Or you might see that you pay out more in essential bills than you bring in every month (in which case, see "Big Decisions vs. Budget Decisions" in order to re-examine your financial priorities and budget).

Either way, the process should be eye-opening and create an awareness of how much money you're spending on a regular basis. Spending is a funny thing; it's often far too easy to open the wallet and pull out the dollars—whether they be in cash, debit card, or credit card—that could be costing you your financial future. The bottom line is that discretionary spending is the money you have control over and can decide how it is best spent.

At this point in the process, people usually go one of a few ways: some want to let old spending habits lie, aren't interested in where the money has been spent, and just want to move on; while some will realize they have been overspending. Still others have the money but aren't paying attention to the timing of bills as they come due, which means that they will overspend in the weeks when there aren't many bills and find themselves in overdraft when the large items need to be paid. Being aware of the timing of the major bills due each month is key to becoming aware of what you really have available to spend each paycheque.

Others, in utter disbelief, want a better understanding of where their money has been going. If you're interested in finding out how the money has been spent, some banks will track every swipe of your debit card and categorize your spending habits for you. This can quickly itemize how much you're spending on restaurants, entertainment, or at retail stores. If your bank doesn't provide this service, a number of free software programs with bank-level encryption will do it for you. If you choose a phone app to do this, make sure it provides bank-level encryption and doesn't allow money transfers. These app companies usually make their money by promoting offers for their advertisers. They will often have a website with a lot of budgeting tools and an app that shows your account balance or tells you if you're running low or need to make a payment, but do your research before using any app that has the ability to link with your bank account. The benefit is that this type of analysis doesn't lie. You can see instantly where your money has been going without having to go through the tedious process of tracking every expenditure for months on end. It can also show trends in spending habits over different periods of time, so if you think this month was exceptionally high for spending costs, you can look back six months or a year to get a more complete picture.

When people look at their bank balance and it's in the black (a positive net balance), they tend to spend the money with little thought of the bills due before the next paycheque. The danger in this behaviour is that when the bills come due, there is not enough money left in the account and they feel that they have to pay with a credit card just to make ends meet. But this whole course of action can be eliminated by knowing what amount is needed to pay the bills in that period and putting it aside so it can't be spent. It's best to begin this process when you've deposited a paycheque. You can write out your expenses before then, but it's harder to jump in during the middle of a pay period. This might also be the case if rent or another big bill is due. It's normal for it to take a month to get your budget up and running because some pay periods have high expenses that eat up most of your paycheque.

FREELANCING FRIEDA

Freelancing Frieda is a single gal who likes the flexibility of working from home and to pick and choose projects in which she's interested. Work–life balance is very important to her, and freelancing creates a lifestyle that gives her a lot more freedom. But because the timing of a freelancer's cash flow is not as consistent as it is for someone with a nine-to-five job, the simple budget becomes even more important for her to gain control of her finances.

If Frieda knows ahead of time when her next project will start/end and the expected billing cycle, she can run her simple budget from project to project. If she does not know when the next project will be, it is important for her to build up a contingency fund of three to six months of living expenses so she doesn't have to rely on her credit card(s) or line of credit during the slower seasons.

STICKING TO YOUR SIMPLE BUDGET

People's needs are fairly straightforward: food, shelter, clothing, transportation. But people often take a wide approach and identify items as a necessity when they are really just a convenience. Wants have a way of making themselves feel like needs. That's why it's so important to look at your stripped-down, bare-bones costs of living. It can also be true that certain items are eating up so much of the whole budget that you really are stuck—you don't have the ability to create any free cash flow. If this is your situation, then in order to free up money, you'll need to take a hard look at the areas consuming so much of your income and make some big decisions around where you live and work or how you commute (see "Big Decisions vs. Budget Decisions" for more detailed guidelines).

For some people, being on a budget can feel like being on a diet. It's restrictive, you feel like you can't have what you want, and you're "hungry" all the time. Ultimately, most people don't stick with a diet over the long run, and can binge when they go off it because they feel like they've been deprived for so long. Personal finances can be exactly the same way. But rather than feeling restricted, why not look at how your choices integrate and how the decisions you make today affect the future. The best diet is the one that makes you feel like you're not on a diet at all and yet it slowly and steadily improves your life and health. It becomes a long-term way of eating rather than a temporary fix. In the same way, your budget becomes a way of living rather than a fiscal band-aid.

If you do want your budget changes to be temporary, however, you can create a debt repayment timeline. It can be helpful to see how long it will take and how much effort needs to be made now.

When you make a decision for yourself, the best advice I can give is to make it sustainable for the duration of the goal you're trying to reach. Some goals will be short-term, like saving for a down payment. Others will need to be permanent, like saving for retirement. You will need to find something that works for you—and doesn't feel like a chore—so that you keep it up for months and years to come.

TALKING ABOUT MONEY WITH
YOUR SIGNIFICANT OTHER

If you and your partner/spouse are in it for the long haul and have combined your incomes, it makes sense to tackle your spending habits as well as your debts together. This can prevent financial situations from getting out of control and keep couples from the blame game that so easily occurs when people begin to feel that their hard work isn't translating into financial success. When a couple initially gets together, they're usually both working and each making enough money to pay their fair share. The bills are likely split 50/50. But as the years go by, circumstances change. What can you do when you love your partner very much but you just can't seem to get ahead because they love ... new shoes or season tickets to their favourite sports team? In the needs-versus-wants discussion, few things can be harder to negotiate than discretionary spending, especially the entertainment budget.

In the early phase of our debt repayment, Cam and I minimized the amount of money that we each got for "fun" because the long-term goal of being debt-free as soon as possible was far more important to us than having nice things now. However, for this type of thinking to work, you need to be able to have the end in sight. Our debt repayment needed to have little progress markers along the way, and for us they were dollar amounts of debt that had been repaid. A major milestone was when we hit the $100,000 repayment mark.

Once we had met certain milestones, our carrying costs on the debt were lower, and we were both comfortable with converting a bit more of our debt repayment money into "fun money."

If a partner insists that he or she needs more money now, they should find a way to earn additional money to feed their spending need or find other non-essential areas of the budget that both partners agree can be trimmed.

The most common argument I tend to hear is, "But I make all the money, so why can't I spend it the way I want?" The bottom line is that, regardless of all the advice in the world, you will spend your money the way you want. So you need to ask yourself, What do I really want? If you want to impress your friends, or satisfy yourself over the short-term with nice things, you are certainly free to do so. You're also free to rack up as much debt as the lenders will give you. But then, further down the road, those choices may leave you with little to show for yourself. When your friends are retiring and travelling, your budget may not allow you to do so. Your future lifestyle is based on the choices you make today. There will be some short-term sacrifices. Cam and I know it first-hand—we've lived with them. But for us, the sacrifices have been well worth it, and we would do it again in a heartbeat to experience the financial freedom we are closer to today. Each couple must make this decision, but ultimately it will come down to you. You must choose which way of living is most important to you.

COMBINING YOUR FINANCES

This can be a touchy subject, but if you and your partner/ spouse have been keeping your finances separate, you may be seeing an incomplete financial picture. It can be significantly easier to run a household and create free cash flow if there are two people and two paycheques working toward the same goal. However, not everyone will be ready to take this step, and not every family lends itself to two paycheques.

Cam and I have always viewed the income we have as "our" money. We had figured out the timeline on our debt repayment, but it was longer than we liked. Neither of us wanted our mortgage to last for twenty-five years because we had so many other ideas about what to do with that money. Since our priorities were aligned, I challenged him with finding an additional way to make income to reduce our payment period. He took me up on the challenge, and while it took a while to find the right fit, toward the end of 2013 he was bringing in additional freelance income by writing articles about stocks for the Motley Fool Canada and then Seeking Alpha in the evenings. Because this didn't happen until nearly the end of a four-year payment period, we hit our marker of over $100,000 in debt repayment without factoring in much additional income. However, since then we've seen the impact the extra cash flow each month has on reaching our goals and we've both become addicted to having the extra money.

The dynamics of a relationship and money management styles can either work for or against a couple. When a couple is in a permanent relationship and starts sharing details about their finances, different attitudes about debt and money management might surface. Here are a few steps to help guide you:

1. Combine bank accounts so that all income is being deposited into one place.

2. Apply the simple budget system to your combined expenses so that both your bills are listed by due date in one place and are accessible to both of you.

3. Have an honest discussion about how much debt you carry and list them all, with the balance owing, interest percentage, minimum payment, and amount of monthly payment.

4. Once the debts are on the table, talk about how often you use your credit cards. The best repayment plan in the world won't get you out of debt if you keep putting it back on as fast as you're paying it off.

5. Decide on the "entertainment budget" you will each get. You won't be accountable to each other for this money, but the other party will have full access to everything else.

If you find that you have more expenses than you do income each month, or if you absolutely can't live without having money in your pocket to spend as discretionary income, there is another way. It involves taking a hard look at the big decisions in your life and creating a lifestyle that you can comfortably afford. However, if you've been living above your means, this method may also require sacrifices. So, before we go any further, now that you know what your monthly fixed costs are, it's time to ask yourself if you're ready to take that hard look at your life and complete the necessary steps in the next section to repay your debt and secure your financial future.

BIG DECISIONS VS. BUDGET DECISIONS

I'm of the opinion that if you take care of your big budget decisions, then the smaller budget decisions, like eating out once in a while or treating yourself, won't have a great impact. In fact, those smaller decisions are all discretionary purchases you can control. You can choose whether to indulge or not. If your budget is tight one week, you may decide not to go out for dinner. On the other hand, if your mortgage's interest rate has gone up a few percentage points by your renewal time, you can't just as easily decide to no longer pay your mortgage. Rather than subjecting yourself to that kind of stress, wouldn't it be easier to make your decisions with the big picture in mind?

Through my work as a financial planner, I have learned that there will always be people who aren't willing to compromise on their day-to-day spending, even if they know it will hurt them over the long run. If you think that describes you, then your decisions involving the big items in your budget can have a substantial impact on your financial well-being. You need to pay special attention to making choices that align and balance all of your priorities, including your current mortgage obligations, with your future retirement plans. This will allow you to manage your big budget items so money is available to pay for your goals.

The following breakdown will help you understand the difference between big decisions and budget decisions:

BIG DECISIONS: The big decisions we make in life are the things we can't necessarily change over the short-term but that have the biggest impact on our budget. These big decisions centre around the items that consume a large percentage of your income, like housing, transportation, and childcare. If your big decisions are made without looking at the big picture (including your career and the income it generates), they can leave you feeling constantly strapped for cash. These big choices will play a large role in how successful you are at reaching your financial goals. The way we make decisions around what we can afford will resonate throughout our whole life, so we need to make choices that will give us the ability to provide an enjoyable lifestyle for ourselves both today and during retirement. The picture of affordability has changed considerably with rising housing costs and stagnant wages. We need a new way to look at things, and *The Debt-Free Lifestyle* holistic approach allows us to do so.

BUDGET DECISIONS: The budget decisions are the choices we make with our available cash flow on a day-to-day basis. My simple budget system teaches you how to separate out what you need each pay period so that you can see clearly the amount of discretionary money you have available. These are short-term decisions, and work best when made on a week-to-week basis, to give you an idea of how much you are able to put toward your goals that week, depending on all the other things that are going on in your life. It also helps to track the results by simply making note of the amount you applied to your goals that week. I use a spreadsheet that is just a continuation of my budget. Once I know how much money I am putting toward my debt, I enter that number for that week of the month. Once you've got it set up, the simple budget shouldn't take more than fifteen minutes to implement every time you get paid.

Then, by combining the impact of your big decisions and budget decisions, you can come up with a workable amount of money that will be available to you on average each month that can be applied to your financial goals.

UNDERSTANDING YOUR DEBTS: Between the mortgage, student loan, line of credit, and credit cards, how much of your income do you think is going toward your debt? If you've recently tried to qualify to buy a house, you'll have found that with current lending rules in Canada, 44% of your gross income can go toward housing and debts.[49] Your gross income is what you make before income taxes and other deductions. The amount that you actually take home, which is called your net income, can be considerably less. If you're maxed out, you've probably already discovered the problem with this—you need to live on the rest. Our debts can take up such a big percentage of our income that managing them properly can have a significant impact on our financial future.

Big decisions, budget decisions, and your debts all need to fit together. The big decisions you make will determine how much cash flow you have available to drive the budget decisions, which ultimately will help you to reach your financial goals. By understanding how lenders treat interest and principal repayments, you can make your own choices about how much of your money you want to see go to the lenders instead of into your own retirement savings.

Sometimes, though, it's still not enough. That's where making more money comes in. Cam and I are both advocates of finding extra work that is enjoyable, plays to your strengths, and is sustainable over the long-term. There are considerable opportunities online these days, if that's your thing. Which brings us to our first Big Decision—your career.

BIG DECISION: CAREER

The most important number in your budget is the amount of money you have coming in each month. Your monthly income needs to be able to meet your lifestyle needs and support your big decisions in a way that is comfortable enough to be sustainable over the long-term and allow room for savings.

After completing the simple budget, some people realize that there is just not enough income to make their lifestyle work. It is also likely that these same people have run up considerable consumer debt, as they have tried to live above their means. If you find yourself in this category, you know all too well that something needs to change. Your lifestyle is not sustainable as it is, and you don't see how you will ever have the money to redirect to financial goals when you are feeling so stuck already.

To reverse this situation, take the following actions:

1. *Change some of your big decisions.*
   If you are willing to make some lifestyle changes, then this section, combined with the simple budget system, will show you how to do so. When you prepare your own simple budget, you will see pretty quickly which areas of your spending are consuming too much of your income and driving the cash flow problems you are experiencing.
2. *Use the simple budget system every time you get paid.*
   Using the simple budget system consistently will ensure you are paying all your bills on time. Budget decisions may be more about generating awareness

of where the dollars that are *not* represented in your allotted budget have been going. The amount of income coming in and your big decisions will have the most impact on how much you are able to do.

3. *Find a way to earn more money.*

   If you aren't willing to make some lifestyle changes—you don't want to compromise spending habits or big decisions about where you live, for example—then your only option is to find a way to make more money. This may mean asking your employer for a raise or working overtime. It may also mean finding a part-time job in the evenings or on weekends, seeking out freelance work you can complete at home, or considering online income-generating opportunities. As I mentioned, on top of his day job, Cam is a freelance writer for Seeking Alpha, which has proven to be interesting extra work that he doesn't have to leave the house for or punch an hour clock to do. Making extra money is also a viable option for people who want to accelerate their financial goals.

Your career choices will drive your lifestyle, and it may be worth your while to endure some short-term fiscal pain to pursue additional education and upgrade your skills and employability. I know I did, and classes in the evening after a long day's work aren't always fun, but it led me to where I am today, and I wouldn't change that for the world. The bottom line is that whatever you choose to do for work, ensure that it's sustainable for the long-term, or at least until you've reached the financial goal you are striving toward.

BIG DECISION: HOUSING

Although income is *the* most important number in your budget, housing is most likely your number-one expense. This one can easily become an emotional decision. People take personal pride in the space they call their own, and it becomes a challenge to balance needs and wants. However, the housing decision can make or break your financial future—especially if you choose to buy rather than rent.

It's no surprise that some areas of the country are becoming more unaffordable than others, and the trade-off between square footage and location is more prevalent than ever. Choosing where to live and what to live in is one of those big decisions that has a ripple effect throughout your finances. Some of your biggest costs are housing and transportation, so these need to be factored in when deciding where to live. It's not just the mortgage payment that can change considerably, it's also the extras, such as the cost of fuel, insurance, and maintenance of your commuter vehicle versus the cost of public transportation. Perhaps it makes sense for you to spend a higher proportion of your budget on housing if you want to correspondingly reduce the amount of time and money you spend on commuting. As we've seen, there are a lot of moving parts that need to fit together to determine what is right for each family. In reality, the housing decision is all about compromise, as there will always be trade-offs in size, location, and many other features.

Condos, apartments, and townhouses

Some people will consult with a mortgage broker and after going through the process realize that they can't afford a freestanding home. The rise of condominium developments, apartments, and townhouses is a testament to the fact that the average family has to find creative ways to get more for their money. The shared costs associated with these types of homes can often get you into an area that you may not have otherwise been able to afford.

People often think that shared living will be a compromise in terms of space or privacy. Yet, all kinds of different developments suit different needs. Before you can even begin to define what home is right for you, you need to determine your priorities. Your choice needs to be a home you can see yourself living in for a good number of years. By coming up with a list before you begin shopping for a home, you ensure that you find a place that is both affordable and a good fit, as opposed to just falling in love with a feature, finish, or characteristic that leaves you way over budget.

What is most important to you?

- Size
- Location
- Cost
- Proximity to a certain school district
- Proximity to downtown
- Distance to work
- How modern/style
- Move-in ready

When you know what you're looking for, it's easier to make the decision when you find it. How do you know if you're getting a good deal? A good place to begin is to put value on some of the trade-offs you will experience by choosing this property. Does proximity to public transit allow you to save money on your commute? Is closer to work and less square footage more desirable than being farther away with more square footage? While it's good to find a match, it needs to match your budget as well. Think of it as a give-and-take. If you can save money in other budget categories, perhaps you'll feel more comfortable taking out a bigger mortgage. But if you can't, be sure to count all the lifestyle costs that will occur as a result of the size and location that you choose.

When Cam and I were looking for our home, we chose Surrey mainly because it was affordable. We'd compared different communities, and basically the farther from Vancouver you got, the more affordable a home would become; the trade-off being the commuting time to work.

If you decide to buy into a shared living arrangement, consider the following factors before you ink the deal:

- Privacy and sound separation
- Good management of the building and grounds
- An action plan and budget for upcoming costs
- A solid contingency fund
- How management handles unexpected expenses: special levies, fee increases
- Long-term financial planning

In the absence of planning, a condominium, apartment, or townhouse complex without an adequate contingency fund will need to rely on special levies paid by the homeowners when something goes wrong. A special levy is a cost that is passed down to the homeowners and earmarked for a particular project. Usually only a few months' notice is given to the owners to get the money together. Ask how your prospective management has handled extraordinary expenses in the past. Is there a plan in place for the wear and tear of different parts of the structure that will naturally occur as the years go by? Knowing what management is inclined to do in the event of an emergency can save you a surprise headache once you've become an owner.

No one likes to see high maintenance fees, but if a complex has kept its fees artificially low and hasn't really been doing much saving, then something has to give. When Cam and I took the helm of the budget process in our complex, we had to raise fees substantially, but in the six years that we have now lived there, we haven't had to issue one special levy. With a bit of creativity, we were able to replace all the roofs with a combined price tag of over $100,000 and do some other substantial repairs. We're now only a couple projects away from being able to save the money the complex has been spending so it can have a comfortable contingency fund. In this way, good building management is a lot like personal financial planning. If you can get your budget under control and create enough free cash flow for upcoming and unexpected expenses, then you'll be fine.

BIG DECISION: TRANSPORTATION

For something as simple as getting from A to B, a wide range of options is available to meet our transportation needs. Right after housing, transportation is often the second expense in a budget that usually gets out of control while being justified as essential.

What's a reasonable cost for transportation? A basic, reliable form of transportation that's suitable to your lifestyle. For example, Mom & Pop Average with their three children need a vehicle that will comfortably fit them all, and any other regular passengers, and that is reliable enough not to be breaking down on a regular basis.

Certain brands of vehicles can be considered status symbols, and some people take great pride in their ability to drive them around. If you and your partner agree that this is something that is important to have and enjoy, then by all means do so. But if it becomes a point of contention between you and your partner, take what would have been the cost of basic, reliable transportation for your situation and subtract it from the cost of the vehicle you want. Anything over the basic amount should come out of your entertainment budget. This kind of advice is especially good for couples who can't agree on what is actually a necessity. The partner who wants the new car will then have to decide if it's worth giving up a part or all of his or her entertainment budget to indulge in that bit of luxury.

Transportation is a big decision because of the amount of the budget it can consume. From the car loan or lease, to fuel, maintenance, and insurance, it is no small cost to drive a vehicle. My car is currently eight years old, and when gas prices in the Lower Mainland began to go up to $1.50 per litre, I switched to public transit. This has kept the mileage on the vehicle low so that I can keep it for a longer period of time. If you find a transit arrangement that is agreeable for you, you might want to free up the cost of fuel, maintenance, and car insurance by giving the car up completely. Car-sharing programs in many metro areas offer low rates that include insurance for those days when you really do need a car to get around.

Another big decision is choosing a place to live that is close to convenient public transportation. Affordability drove our initial housing decision, but having a public transit route nearby is something to keep in mind when you are looking for a new home. Having this option available can free up a good amount of cash flow that can be used to accelerate other goals. We are also advocates of owning a car outright and doing proper maintenance so that it can be kept as long as possible. Once the monthly car payment is gone, this significant amount of cash can be directed elsewhere.

BIG DECISION: CHILDCARE

When Mom & Pop Average first met, they talked about their hopes and dreams and were delighted to find out they both wanted a big family. After their son and daughter were born, they still felt that the family wasn't quite complete, so they had one more child, a bubbly little girl. While their family is their primary source of joy and satisfaction, their financial situation was changing.

While Mom was on maternity leave, her income was considerably less than what she was used to. As much as she loved the idea of staying home to raise the kids, when her maternity leave was up, she was faced with the need to go back to work and pay for childcare. In addition to baby food, toys, diapers, and the clothes the kids kept growing out of, childcare took a huge bite out of the money they would have otherwise had available in their budget. After baby number three, Mom took a year off after her maternity leave to keep childcare costs down and because she felt that spending time with the children was the most meaningful work she could do. They had kept some of the clothes and toys from their first and second child to reuse, but Mom and Pop Average learned that they needed to have a strong handle on their budget to make it all work.

After Mom went back to work, Mom & Pop Average decided that their next big goal would be to own a house of their own. They were beginning to feel cramped in the apartment they had been renting and wanted a house big enough for all three kids where they could make a lifetime of family memories. Pop took on a few extra shifts while Mom, now working full-time again, looked for ways to cut costs so they could save for a down payment.

Young families have to adjust their budgets to the increased costs that come with having children, and yet when it's time to go back to work and the daycare options are examined, many couples find that daycare costs can be prohibitively high. Some parents find that they would be left with only a few hundred dollars if they went back to work and paid for daycare. In living wage studies for families of four, when it is assumed that one child is in full-time care and the other is in before- and after-school daycare, a sample budget published by the Huffington Post[50] showed a childcare cost of $1,324 per month in Metro Vancouver. During that period of time, childcare was the second-largest cost for the family, after housing.

Having children is a wonderful thing, and it is certainly a big decision that impacts future plans. With RESPs and increased costs, families can find that in the years before school when care costs are the highest, they may need to reprioritize some of their long-term goals to put family first. This could simply mean waiting a few years until the kids are in school to start a major savings project. It is well worth it, though, as raising good kids with family values is one of the greatest contributions that can be made to society and our collective future.

BUDGET DECISION: FOOD

In my home I'm especially lucky because, thanks to our division of domestic labour, my husband does nearly all of the cooking. In the seemingly endless cycle of always being busy, it is far too easy for the cooking routine to become one of convenience. In our mid-twenties, we were buying and eating mostly frozen food that could be popped in the oven for twenty minutes. We knew that the processed food cost more than the fresh stuff, so we made the switch in order to save money and then felt healthier to boot! We even found a local veggie store that sold fresh produce at a lower cost than the big-box grocer. As part of the switch to a healthier diet that includes fresh fruits, vegetables, and meat, we had to learn to meal plan. When we go on our weekly grocery run, we buy just enough food to get us through to the next week. This keeps us from having to throw away good food gone bad and takes some of the stress out of cooking because we know what we're going to have ahead of time.

BUDGET DECISION:
MEALS ON THE RUN = ENTERTAINMENT

What happens when the alarm rings and it's the third time you've hit snooze. You peer at the clock. If you get up now, there's just enough time to brush your teeth, make yourself presentable, and run out the door to make it to work on time. Breakfast and lunch were never meant to be meals on the go, and it's not good for your body or your pocketbook. If you spend $5 on breakfast and $15 on lunch every day, $400 a month is gone before you know it. This is not news to anyone. The ever-popular "cut the latte habit" mantra has found its way into mainstream culture, but judging by what I see out of my office window every day, it hasn't seemed to stop the line at our local Tim Hortons from reaching right out the front door.

We deal with this in two ways: First, by limiting the amount of money in our bank account, we know we have to stick to a set food budget. If we decide to spend money eating out, for me that comes out of the entertainment budget. If I really feel like I just can't resist a special treat, I'll take it out of my personal entertainment budget so that I can indulge guilt-free. This also makes me give thought to the other ways I could be spending the money and to decide if the food is what I really want (it usually is). We have more leeway now, but since we didn't have much wiggle room when we began, we needed to learn to make all three meals of the day fit easily into our budget.

It's a bit boring, I admit, but, along with a healthier life-style, we decided that the only way we could get around the early morning rush was to have our lunches prepared ahead of time. I got into the habit of pulling out the slow cooker every Sunday afternoon. In a slow cooker, you can buy cheaper cuts of meat and let them tenderize all day; we've made soups, chicken, chili, meatballs, and other dishes. As long as you don't mind a bit of repetition, you can have lunches ready for the week. So when that alarm rings for the third time, grabbing a pre-made meal on your way out the door takes very little time or effort.

It's true that too much of the same routine can get tedious. The same soup five times a week can get a bit hard to swallow. Sometimes you need to get out of the house and have an evening out. For years, when we did go out, we wouldn't order alcohol with dinner to keep the bill down, but again, anything like that should be viewed as part of the entertainment budget and not the food budget.

Whenever I find myself in downtown Vancouver, regardless of the day of the week, the restaurants always seem to be full of people. In some cases, there are so many people eating out that meals are sold pretty cheap. If dinner out costs less than buying the ingredients and cooking them yourself, then go nuts, but make sure that inexpensive food doesn't come at the compromise of your health.

WHAT WILL YOUR DEBT-FREE LIFESTYLE LOOK LIKE?

The big decisions and the budget decisions you make will be as unique as you are. You can think of the big decisions and the budget decisions as the process of building your lifestyle. From housing, childcare, and transportation to food and entertainment, making cohesive choices will reduce financial stress and make your long-term goals achievable. There is give-and-take in every major life decision, and the purpose should always be to create a balance that you enjoy and can see yourself doing over the long-term.

three

THE MORTGAGE COMMITMENT

HOW MUCH CAN YOU AFFORD?

The home plays such an important role in our lives as a gathering place, where memories are made and conversations are shared. It is often the asset that is passed down from generations as part of our legacy. The old adage holds true: there really is no place like home.

But the decision of where and what we will call home is a changing conversation based on both income and affordability challenges. When the housing decision is made, the choice will ripple through our finances for a lifetime because it's most often the largest expense in our budget and one of our longest obligations. We create our lifestyle around what we have left once the big-ticket items (like the mortgage) are paid. If we've taken on too much, cash flow will be tight now and it will hinder our ability to save for the future. We need to find new ways to make the most out of what we have. This is done by challenging conventional wisdom and using the way a mortgage is structured to our advantage. But first let's start with how we get a mortgage to begin with.

When Cam and I went in to qualify for our mortgage, I was nervous. How did they make the decision about whether we could get a mortgage, and more importantly, how did they decide how much? We knew our incomes weren't anything to get too excited about, but they were average. We were young and hard-working. At the time, we had credit cards and a line of credit, which had been run up and paid down. We'd always paid our bills on time and our credit scores were good. But what does that mean? Is it enough?

In Canada, lending rules are in place to ensure we don't overextend ourselves. As frustrating as it can be when we're trying to qualify for a home, the rules really are there for our protection. Without them, we could take on more than we are able to pay back and, in a worst-case scenario, lose the house as a result. As a homeowner, you want to do everything in your power to make sure that you never get to this point.

HOW TO QUALIFY FOR A MORTGAGE

Qualifying for your mortgage will depend on a number of factors, including your credit score and repayment history, employment record, income, down payment, other assets and liabilities, character, and capacity to repay the loan as well as making sure your level of income passes certain fitness tests.[51] This chapter comes with a big caveat: the underwriting guidelines that each lender uses are not publicly available and can change at any time. The following guidelines are provided by the B.C. mortgage broker's course manual and by the Office of the Superintendent of Financial Institutions (OSFI), which was formed by the Government of Canada to regulate federal financial institutions and which reports to the Minister of Finance as an independent agency.[52]

Loan-to-value ratio

The loan-to-value ratio determines what percentage of your property is being financed. It's essentially a test of collateral: the lender wants you to have equity, or skin in the game, because they don't want you to be in a position where they have to foreclose on the house. If you are a first-time buyer, you can initially control this loan-to-value ratio with the size of your down payment. A big down payment is your best protection. It builds automatic flexibility, and it also means that once you get over 20%, you won't have to pay the mortgage loan insurance premium. Canada Mortgage and Housing Corporation (CMHC)'s mortgage loan insurance program has premiums that will decrease as your loan-to-value ratio decreases.[53] This means that the more you put down upfront, the less you will have to pay in a mortgage loan insurance premium. If mortgage loan insurance is to be factored in because you have less than 20% down, the premium is rolled into the mortgage as a lump payment. It will not affect the loan-to-value ratio, but it will affect the debt service ratios.[54]

As time goes on, your loan-to-value ratio will decrease as you pay down your mortgage and as your home increases in value. Decreases are good because this means that you have more equity in your home. Increases in your home's value are additional protection against interest rate increases because more equity will give you greater flexibility when interest rates increase if you do need to refinance.

Mortgage insurance

It also bears mentioning that mortgage loan insurance is purely for the benefit of the lender. It does not protect you in any way. However, because it pays the lender in the event of default, lenders are able to offer lower mortgage rates than they would have otherwise been able to if they had to factor those defaults into the price.[55] As a homeowner, you should take a look at getting a personal life insurance policy and a disability insurance policy. The life insurance protects your family's finances in the unexpected event of death, and a disability policy protects your ability to continue to pay your bills if you cannot work due to an accident or illness. Both are crucial parts of managing risk.

When you are approved for your mortgage, your lender will offer you mortgage life insurance. This is different from the mortgage loan insurance that can be required based on your loan-to-value ratio. Don't take the insurance offered by the bank until you are aware of the differences between the plans offered by the bank and those offered through an independent insurance advisor. An individual life insurance policy from an independent advisor is superior to the mortgage life insurance you would get from the bank in four ways:

First, the death benefit goes directly to your beneficiary, presumably your partner/spouse, and the beneficiary can then decide how best to use the money. Mortgage life insurance through the bank will go directly toward discharging the mortgage.

Second, with the policy at the bank, as the years go by and your mortgage decreases, the amount of coverage through the insurance will also decrease, but your premium payments for the coverage will stay the same. With an individual policy, your beneficiary would receive the whole amount that was originally applied for. That means if you've got a $1,000,000 policy and there is only $50,000 left on your mortgage at the time of death, through the bank policy the $50,000 mortgage would be discharged, and that's it. Through the individual policy, your beneficiary would receive a $1,000,000![56]

Third, with an individual policy your health is assessed at the time of application. Once it is approved, the coverage is yours. With mortgage life insurance, your health is checked after you pass away.[57] That means that your beneficiary not only has to deal with your passing but also has to substantiate that your health was good at the time of application—and that could have been over twenty years prior! *CBC Marketplace* did a great exposé on this in 2008, and it's worth looking up. Your best defence is to find an independent insurance broker who will be able to guide you through this process. Finally, an independent broker should be contracted with all the major insurance companies in Canada to find you the best product and price for your needs.

Debt service ratios

A lender will be looking at two ratios: one measures the costs associated with housing and asks if you can afford to make your mortgage payments, plus some other basic housing expenses. As mentioned in Chapter 1, this ratio is called the gross debt service ratio (GDSR). Because you may carry other debts that are not housing related, a second ratio was created to look at housing plus your total debt load. This one exists to make sure that you can handle all the loans in your life, be they car loans, credit cards, personal lines of credit, and any other interest-bearing vehicle that you can think of. The ratio that measures everything together is called the total debt service ratio (TDSR).

Both ratios are based on your gross income. Your gross annual salary is the amount you agreed to work for when you accepted your employment. It is what you earn before taxes or other deductions are made. It's also worth mentioning that lenders can vary how they interpret "gross income." It is common to take a two-year average of the income of both people on title, including overtime, which may make payments more difficult if that overtime is not continued. In addition, 50% to 100% of regular investment income can be considered. Government legislation and lender policies can also impact the actual ratios used, and they can change at any time.[58]

But what does this mean for average folks like you and me? In our case, if I signed an employment contract for $40,000 and my husband signed one for $38,000, our gross family income would be $78,000. That means that our gross monthly income would be $6,500, which is found by simply taking both of our incomes and dividing them by the twelve months in a year. Keep in mind that this is not the actual amount we take home every month, but it is the amount the lenders will use to form their decision.

The lenders are looking at the two ratios when you apply, so let's break them down in greater detail. The first one is the GDSR, which according to the CMHC shouldn't exceed 35% of your gross family income.[59] This means that with our gross monthly income of $6,500, no more than $2,275 a month should be going toward servicing our mortgage and its associated costs.

The formula to calculate your GDSR is:

$$\frac{\text{Principal} + \text{Interest} + \text{Taxes} + \text{Heat}}{\text{Gross Annual Family Income}}$$

The principal and the interest is the blend that you'll see in your mortgage payment. This also includes any mortgage loan insurance premiums that will apply if your down payment is less than 20%. Heating costs, property taxes, and 50% of a maintenance fee, if applicable, can be included as well.

The second ratio is the TDSR, which starts off the same as the GDSR and calculates your housing costs, but then also takes into account all the other forms of debt you have: credit cards, lines of credit, and car loans. The formula to calculate your TDSR is:

$$\frac{\text{Principal} + \text{Interest} + \text{Taxes} + \text{Heat} + \text{Other Debt Obligations}}{\text{Gross Annual Family Income}}$$

According to this ratio, no more than 42% of your gross income should be going toward your total debt. The total amount Cam and I can put toward housing and debt on a monthly basis using this ratio is $2,730.

One concern with these ratios is that they use family income *before* taxes and deductions are taken off, which means that you are qualifying based on an amount of income that is greater than what you are actually taking home. After taxes and other deductions like pension contributions or extended health benefits, what you take home will be much less. This is called our net amount. When we began, my $1,200 every two weeks meant my net income was closer to $31,200 a year. With Cam bringing home $2,200 a month and me bringing home $2,400, ours was a combined net income of $4,600 a month, which is the amount that is actually available in our bank account to spend. This is our real-life example, but your net number will vary based on the amount you earn and the benefits you receive at work.

If the ratios were based on net income instead of gross income, what percentage of our take-home income would Cam and I be spending on our debt and housing costs?

MONTHLY INCOME: $6,500		
	% OF GROSS FAMILY INCOME	% OF NET FAMILY INCOME
Gross Debt Service Ratio	35%	49%
Total Debt Service Ratio	42%	59%

This means that when we're qualifying for a mortgage, housing plus the costs to service our other debts shouldn't be over 42% of our gross income. After taxes and other deductions, we will actually end up spending nearly 60% of our take-home income on debt and housing alone! With this much of our income going toward debt and housing, you can see how families like ours are finding it difficult to pay all our other bills on the amount that is left over!

When we're trying hard to make ends meet, we often think that if we just made more money, life would be easier and we would get all our bills under control. However, a Statistics Canada report (2012)[60] showed that debt has a tendency to go up with income. The following example of household debt represents mortgage, and consumer debt, and the income is before-tax income.

HOUSEHOLD INCOME	AMOUNT OF DEBT	% OF THE TOTAL DEBT
Under $ 50,000	$ 57,700	13%
$ 50,000–$ 99,999	$ 95,400	31%
$ 100,000 and over	$ 172,400	56%

Why is this so? We make our big decisions such as housing based largely on what the banks are willing to lend us. Since everyone wants to feel they got the best they could afford, it's human nature to take as much as we are able.

Since the income tax schedule in Canada is progressive, it can actually be more challenging for people with higher incomes to get ahead if they choose to take out the biggest mortgage and largest loans that the lenders are willing to give them. This is because the amount of tax they owe increases as their earnings increase. With a higher income, they will qualify for a larger mortgage and other loans, but the percentage they get to keep gets smaller as more of what they make gets paid out as tax in the higher income tax brackets. This leaves less money to service those loans and pay for the other day-to-day living expenses.

Income

Cam and I live in British Columbia, so when we're looking at our tax rate, we look at the combined federal and B.C. provincial rates. In 2009, Cam's income of $38,000 was just above the threshold for the combined bracket of 20.06%. In fact, both of our top tax brackets that year didn't exceed 22.70%. Compare that to one person working and earning our combined income of $78,000, with a top combined federal and provincial tax bracket of 32.50%,[61] and he or she is paying considerably more taxes on the same amount of money than we were. From this point of view, couples with both spouses working can find themselves in an advantageous position, as both partners get to take advantage of paying tax at a lower rate as they move up through the tax schedule.

The higher your income, the larger the gap between your gross and net income. This means that you will have to spend a bigger percentage of your net income to make the payments you qualified for. So even though we all qualify using the same ratios, the person with the higher income may actually be at a disadvantage because of the difference going toward taxes. This also means that there will be much less money going toward life because it is being eaten up by higher payments that you thought you would be able to sustain because you qualified for them!

This brings us to an interesting dilemma.

Let's catch up with our friends, Mom & Pop Average and Mr. Metro. Mom & Pop Average have a mortgage balance of $450,000, which is in line with the average Canadian housing price, and Mr. Metro has a mortgage with a balance outstanding of $1,000,000, close to the average house price in a bustling metropolitan area.

Mom & Pop Average

Like us, Mom & Pop Average both work at average-paying jobs. Because they have two incomes, they both get to take advantage of the lower tax brackets as well as the basic personal amount[62] both federally and provincially. They live in Winnipeg, so their taxes reflect the Manitoba tax schedule. Mom & Pop Average went to qualify for a house before reading this book, so the TDSR of 42% of their gross income was used. Since they didn't have any other debt, their family income of $86,932 allowed them to qualify for the $450,000 mortgage, with an interest rate of 4%. If the lower GDSR of 35% of their gross family income had been used, they would have needed a household income of $100,890 to qualify for the same mortgage at 4% interest, all else being equal.

MOM & POP AVERAGE	FAMILY INCOME	TAXES[63]
Mom Average's Income	$ 41,252	$ 8,157
Pop Average's Income	$ 45,680	$ 9,455
Combined Income	$ 86,932	$ 17,612

		% OF GROSS INCOME	% OF AFTER TAX INCOME
Combined Gross Monthly Income	$ 7,244		
Monthly Taxes	$ 1,468		
Monthly After Tax Income	$ 5,776		
Gross Debt Service Ratio	$ 2,535	35%	44%
Total Debt Service Ratio	$ 3,042	42%	53%

Mr. Metro

When Mr. Metro was married, Mrs. Metro didn't work. Like Mom & Pop Average, Mr. Metro took out the biggest mortgage he could, but that was many years ago and his mortgage amount has now decreased. He lives in Toronto. His $180,925 of income is what he would now need to qualify for a $1,000,000 mortgage at a 4% interest rate using the TDSR of 42%.

MR. METRO	FAMILY INCOME	TAXES[64]
Mr. Metro's Income	$ 180,925	$ 63,007

		% OF GROSS INCOME	% OF AFTER TAX INCOME
Monthly Income	$ 15,077		
Monthly Taxes	$ 5,250		
Monthly After Tax Income	$ 9,827		
Gross Debt Service Ratio	$ 5,277	35%	54%
Total Debt Service Ratio	$ 6,332	42%	64%

Can you see how Mr. Metro, in spite of his great salary, finds himself in a tight spot because of the taxes owing on the salary and that income being earned and taxed on one person? Both families qualified for their respective homes based on 42% of gross income, but there was a significantly higher level of pressure put on Mr. Metro's pocketbook. If housing and debt service takes up 64% of Mr. Metro's take-home income, it means he has only 36% left to spend on everything else! And these calculations are looking at tax only, and don't factor in other deductions like pension, union dues, and things that can vary considerably from person to person, leaving you with even less to take home. In addition, the percentages used in the lending ratios, while regulated, have been increasing over the years as housing across Canada has become more expensive.

Knowing what we know now, and seeing how much pressure tax can put on our pocketbook, how much house is right for you? While the affordability ratio can get you into a home, it may not be the right fit if it ends up eating up so much of your take-home income that you're finding it difficult to pay the bills on a daily basis. If Mr. Metro was a first-time homebuyer, he may have wanted to look at a home that was less than his lenders were willing to give him so he could have had enough income remaining to sustain his lifestyle and save for other goals.

The other point that bears mentioning is that when the lenders calculate the gross and total debt service ratios, they don't take into account all the costs related to your housing. This is why I think you should do two affordability calculations. The first is the way the lenders will do it, so you can see what you could potentially qualify for. The second will take a look at the true costs, so you can see how much you can actually afford.

To calculate your true costs, you need to look at your "sunk costs," which are any expenses needed to own the home and to maintain it. These are essentially your costs of living, but I call them "sunk" because while you need to spend that amount to live, it does not build equity. Only principal repayments reduce the debt you have and build your equity.

Cam & I

Let's take a look at the numbers when we bought our home. The lender would use the following to calculate our gross and total debt service ratios (our monthly maintenance fee at the time was $267, but the lender would use only half of this amount in the calculation):

	ANNUAL	MONTHLY
Property Taxes	$ 1,307	$ 109.00
Heating (approx.)	$ 550	$ 46.00
Maintenance Fee	$ 1,602	$ 133.50
Total:	$ 3,459	$ 288.50

For the lender using the GDSR calculation, these additional costs of $289 a month form part of the $2,275 per month, or 35% of our gross family income allocated to housing. That means that with a GDSR of $2,275, if Cam & I want to keep our housing costs within 35% of our before-tax income, we would want our mortgage payment to be no more than $1,986.

Next, we did the calculation again, with all the main costs associated with living:

	ANNUAL	MONTHLY
Property Taxes	$ 1,307	$ 109.00
Heating	$ 550	$ 46.00
Water	$ 408	$ 34.00
Contents Insurance	$ 420	$ 35.00
Maintenance Fee	$ 3,204	$ 267.00
	$ 5,889	$ 491.00

By this calculation, the amount that needs to be taken into consideration for our actual affordability is $491 a month, which is $200 a month higher than we were led to believe using just the debt service ratio.

Now, when we look at how much of a mortgage payment we can afford, we need to be able to add in the full amount of our costs, and still need to try to keep it within the 35% GDSR. What does this mean for us? To keep within the 35% of gross income per month, our monthly mortgage payment now shouldn't exceed $1,784 if we want all our costs to be included, instead of the $1,986 that the lending ratio suggested. We can amend this further if we want to add in ongoing maintenance expenses as well.

How much can you actually afford?

As you can see, the amount you qualify for and the amount you can comfortably afford may be very different numbers. Taking on a mortgage that is larger than what you can actually handle can make the rest of your cash flow really tight and significantly limit your ability to reach other financial goals. Housing is an important part of everyone's budget, but it shouldn't take up so much that it strictly limits what you have left to spend on everything else. If it does, those extra dollars every month could be costing you the ability to save for a comfortable retirement. While having a house going into retirement is hugely beneficial, you have to look at the true costs and opportunity costs so that you don't end up overpaying when interest rates are high or, worse, you are no longer able to afford your home if your payment goes up and your budget doesn't have anything left to cut.

What if you've taken on too much?

If you are worried that you may have taken on too much, there are some silver linings. Time can have a major impact on the actual outcome.

First, your mortgage payments will only change a limited number of times over the mortgage's lifetime. The amount that it can change is based on the length of term you selected. If you have chosen a five-year term with a fixed rate then there are five times during the twenty-five-year length of your mortgage for payments to adjust.

The Bank of Canada recognizes the risks associated with Canadians being so highly leveraged.[65] In fact, that's why interest rates have been so low for so long. The Bank of Canada is well aware that an additional dollar going toward the mortgage cannot be spent elsewhere in the economy, and that people's cash flow is strapped as it is. For that reason, a slow rate increase would ease consumers back to normalized rates, but the only thing that would reduce the problem is if highly leveraged homebuyers are able to reduce the principal owing on their mortgages to an amount that will be sustainable when interest rates rise. That can be done by following this program, or by choosing a home that is priced lower than the maximum you qualify for. If enough time passes, you may be able to pay down sufficient principal to keep the payments manageable. The further you are into your mortgage, the smaller the amount of principal you will have outstanding and the lower the impact when interest rates do rise.

Higher rates will also have the impact of reducing the number of first-time buyers who would have qualified under a lower rate but who would need a higher salary to qualify for the same mortgage once rates have increased. This could also mean that fewer homes will change hands as affordability gets further out of reach for those who do not yet own a home.

Also, your income should increase over the course of your career. Once your income exceeds the amount that was originally used in the debt service ratios you qualified with, your ratio would decrease. The practical application to this is that you would have more money available to spend on housing if the need arises.

The highest risk is for those who have just bought a home and have high loan-to-value ratios, meaning that they hold very little equity in the property and are at the beginning of the amortization schedule where they will not be paying down principal very quickly. This risk can also hold true for those who have refinanced, but if their home has increased in value or their salary has increased, they may still be able to find additional cash flow to make extra payments to mitigate the risk of higher mortgage payments due to interest rate increases. The impact of rising interest rates may not be immediate, as mortgages with variable rates would feel it first, but as terms began to renew, we would see the trickle-through effect of less money being spent elsewhere in the economy as it needs to go toward the mortgage.

CHOOSING THE RIGHT HOME—AND THE MORTGAGE TO GO WITH IT

Choosing the right home for you depends on so many things, like where you decide to live and what your other costs will be. If you choose to live close to a metropolitan area and can take public transit, that decision will save money on transportation. The simple budget system from earlier now serves two purposes: not only has it helped with your week-to-week cash flow, but it will also give you a needs-based idea of how much of a mortgage you can afford to take on. If you add up all the essentials on your list, excluding the mortgage but including food and entertainment, and calculate what percentage of your net income you need for those, you can easily see the maximum mortgage you can take on comfortably without feeling behind the eight ball all the time.

What is the right house for you? It's a home with a mortgage payment that fits comfortably within your budget—and also leaves you enough room to save for the future. Having some wiggle room will become important because interest rates will go up at some point in the future. Depending on how far you are into your mortgage, this can have a real impact on the dollar amount you have to pay out each month. One of the best things you can do for yourself is to prepay early on in your mortgage, or take on a smaller mortgage to begin with.

WHAT IF I CAN'T AFFORD TO BUY A HOME?

There will be a base amount that you'll have to attribute to the cost of living somewhere. Look at the amount of your budget that is currently going toward rent and calculate that percentage of your gross and net income. Renting is not regulated in the same way that buying a home is because your contract with your landlord is a private one, and there is no large sum of money being borrowed. If you can't pay your rent, your landlord can evict you, but a lender has taken on a much bigger risk. Because of the lack of regulation, renters with lower incomes may have far more than the 44% of gross income that homeowners can have going toward debt and housing. If you decide that home ownership is a worthwhile goal for you, you may need to look at your big decisions and make some temporary compromises around size or location so that you have enough cash flow to save for a down payment. The size of your down payment also plays a large role in how much you can afford, but if you're wanting to get into a home quickly and don't mind paying the mortgage loan insurance premium, you can buy a home under a million dollars with 5% down.

If there's still not enough room in your budget, you'll have to consider other big decisions. Look at the other big-ticket items consuming a large percentage of your income. If there is consumer debt, focus on paying it down first. If there is a young child in daycare, perhaps you'll need to wait until he or she is in school to free up some cash flow there. The bottom line is, stick with your simple budget system each week and follow these three steps:

1. Pay off your consumer debt first.
2. Re-allocate the amount you are saving on debt/interest to your savings.
3. Save, save, save!

You will be surprised at how much of a difference a large down payment will make in terms of housing affordability. Perhaps the home you wanted is in the future, just a few years of saving down the road.

four

PAY IT OFF!

USE YOUR MORTGAGE PAYMENTS TO YOUR ADVANTAGE

Have you ever wondered why your mortgage was designed to last twenty-five years? We saw earlier that the amount of interest you pay is based on the interest rate and that you can pay considerably more than the value of your home over a twenty-five-year period when interest rates are high. We know that our mortgage is often our biggest expense, and we know that a lot of the money goes to interest. This can result in a lost opportunity, as the money could have been spent in other ways, such as securing our retirement.

So why does your mortgage take that long? And how do you go about making sure that you pay as little interest as possible?

Mortgages are what we call amortized loans, and what makes them special is the way the principal and interest are blended. A mortgage is structured so that for the first part of the mortgage, the bulk of your payment goes toward interest. If you've taken out a new mortgage and have been paying it down for a few years, that's why you haven't seen much equity being built up. Then, in the later years of the mortgage, as your mortgage balance declines, more principal is repaid than interest. The amount of time that it will take for you to make more principal repayments than interest payments will depend on the interest rate you have been paying. A lower interest rate will let you get to increase principal repayment in a shorter span of time than a high interest rate would allow. But if taking the full twenty-five years is too long for you because you want to move on to your other financial goals, this structure creates a unique opportunity.

MOM & POP AVERAGE

What if Mom & Pop Average's mortgage of $450,000 had a level interest rate of 8% throughout the whole twenty-five years to show the pure effect of the amortization schedule without the influence of changing rates? The payment is $3,434.46, and it's paid monthly with interest compounded semi-annually. This is what their amortization schedule would look like:

| YEAR | MORTGAGE AMOUNT | INTEREST RATE | ANNUAL PAYMENT | ANNUAL PRINCIPAL | INTEREST PAYABLE | |
					ANNUAL	CUMULATIVE
1	$ 443,987	8%	$ 41,124	$ 6,013	$ 35,200	$ 35,200
2	$ 437,483	8%	$ 41,124	$ 6,504	$ 34,710	$ 69,910
3	$ 430,449	8%	$ 41,124	$ 7,034	$ 34,179	$ 104,089
4	$ 422,840	8%	$ 41,124	$ 7,608	$ 33,605	$ 137,694
5	$ 414,611	8%	$ 41,124	$ 8,229	$ 32,984	$ 170,679
6	$ 405,710	8%	$ 41,124	$ 8,901	$ 32,313	$ 202,991
7	$ 396,083	8%	$ 41,124	$ 9,627	$ 31,586	$ 234,578
8	$ 385,670	8%	$ 41,124	$ 10,413	$ 30,801	$ 265,378
9	$ 374,408	8%	$ 41,124	$ 11,262	$ 29,951	$ 295,330
10	$ 362,227	8%	$ 41,124	$ 12,181	$ 29,032	$ 324,362
11	$ 349,051	8%	$ 41,124	$ 13,175	$ 28,038	$ 352,400
12	$ 334,801	8%	$ 41,124	$ 14,251	$ 26,963	$ 379,363
13	$ 319,387	8%	$ 41,124	$ 15,413	$ 25,800	$ 405,163
14	$ 302,716	8%	$ 41,124	$ 16,671	$ 24,542	$ 429,705
15	$ 284,685	8%	$ 41,124	$ 18,031	$ 23,182	$ 452,888
16	$ 265,182	8%	$ 41,124	$ 19,503	$ 21,711	$ 474,598
17	$ 244,088	8%	$ 41,124	$ 21,094	$ 20,119	$ 494,718
18	$ 221,272	8%	$ 41,124	$ 22,816	$ 18,398	$ 513,116
19	$ 196,595	8%	$ 41,124	$ 24,677	$ 16,536	$ 529,652
20	$ 169,904	8%	$ 41,124	$ 26,691	$ 14,523	$ 544,174
21	$ 141,035	8%	$ 41,124	$ 28,869	$ 12,345	$ 556,519
22	$ 109,811	8%	$ 41,124	$ 31,225	$ 9,989	$ 566,508
23	$ 76,038	8%	$ 41,124	$ 33,773	$ 7,441	$ 573,949
24	$ 39,511	8%	$ 41,124	$ 36,528	$ 4,685	$ 578,634
25	$ 0	8%	$ 41,124	$ 39,510	$ 1,704	$ 580,339

If you look at the breakdown between principal and interest, you'll notice that it takes until Year 17 for more of the mortgage payment to go toward principal instead of interest! The amount of time it will take to get to the place where you're paying more principal down than interest will depend on the interest rate and the amount of payment you're making relative to the balance outstanding on the mortgage.

This is where it gets interesting: Think of the interest you must pay on your mortgage as the hurdle you have to jump over in order to get ahead. In an amortization schedule, the hurdle is highest in the early years, and then it gets lower as time goes on. The amount of mortgage you take on will be the first determining factor in how high the hurdle is. The interest rate will be the second. Interest is a sunk cost—it is truly lost—but there is a way to get around it and accelerate your efforts. Reducing the amount of principal you owe will significantly affect the total amount of payments you make and as a result reduce the total interest costs and the length of time it will take to pay off your mortgage. When you make a prepayment, instead of having to jump over that hurdle, you get to walk around it, as prepayments bypass the amortization schedule and get added directly to paying off the principal and building equity.

The interest rate is something that is out of your control, so let's focus on the things you can control. In addition to your interest rate, the amount of your mortgage and the length of time you take to pay it down are two of the most important factors in your quest to become debt-free.

Here's what Mom & Pop Average's mortgage repayment would have looked like if there were a 4% interest rate the whole way through. Their monthly payment would be: $2,367.09.

YEAR	MORTGAGE AMOUNT	INTEREST RATE	ANNUAL PAYMENT	ANNUAL PRINCIPAL	INTEREST PAYABLE	
					ANNUAL	CUMULATIVE
1	$ 439,253	4%	$ 28,405	$ 10,747	$ 17,658	$ 17,658
2	$ 428,071	4%	$ 28,405	$ 11,181	$ 17,224	$ 34,881
3	$ 416,438	4%	$ 28,405	$ 11,633	$ 16,772	$ 51,653
4	$ 404,335	4%	$ 28,405	$ 12,103	$ 16,302	$ 67,955
5	$ 391,743	4%	$ 28,405	$ 12,592	$ 15,813	$ 83,768
6	$ 378,642	4%	$ 28,405	$ 13,101	$ 15,304	$ 99,072
7	$ 365,012	4%	$ 28,405	$ 13,630	$ 14,775	$ 113,847
8	$ 350,831	4%	$ 28,405	$ 14,181	$ 14,224	$ 128,071
9	$ 336,077	4%	$ 28,405	$ 14,754	$ 13,651	$ 141,723
10	$ 320,727	4%	$ 28,405	$ 15,350	$ 13,055	$ 154,778
11	$ 304,757	4%	$ 28,405	$ 15,970	$ 12,435	$ 167,213
12	$ 288,142	4%	$ 28,405	$ 16,615	$ 11,790	$ 179,003
13	$ 270,856	4%	$ 28,405	$ 17,286	$ 11,119	$ 190,122
14	$ 252,871	4%	$ 28,405	$ 17,985	$ 10,420	$ 200,542
15	$ 234,160	4%	$ 28,405	$ 18,711	$ 9,694	$ 210,236
16	$ 214,693	4%	$ 28,405	$ 19,467	$ 8,938	$ 219,174
17	$ 194,439	4%	$ 28,405	$ 20,254	$ 8,151	$ 227,325
18	$ 173,367	4%	$ 28,405	$ 21,072	$ 7,333	$ 234,659
19	$ 151,444	4%	$ 28,405	$ 21,923	$ 6,482	$ 241,140
20	$ 128,635	4%	$ 28,405	$ 22,809	$ 5,596	$ 246,737

					INTEREST PAYABLE	
YEAR	MORTGAGE AMOUNT	INTEREST RATE	ANNUAL PAYMENT	ANNUAL PRINCIPAL	ANNUAL	CUMULATIVE
21	$ 104,905	4%	$ 28,405	$ 23,730	$ 4,675	$ 251,411
22	$ 80,215	4%	$ 28,405	$ 24,689	$ 3,716	$ 255,127
23	$ 54,529	4%	$ 28,405	$ 25,687	$ 2,718	$ 257,846
24	$ 27,804	4%	$ 28,405	$ 26,724	$ 1,681	$ 259,526
25	$ 0	4%	$ 28,405	$ 27,804	$ 601	$ 260,127

In this case, the low interest rates allow the principal to start exceeding the interest portion in Year 9, but even so the mortgage will still stretch out to last the full twenty-five years. How can this be? Shouldn't the low interest rate allow you to pay down your mortgage faster?

The answer lies in the amortization schedule. If you signed up for a twenty-five-year amortization period, the lender will structure the loan so that it lasts for all of those twenty-five years. It does this by adjusting the payment amount. The amortization schedule in itself is not bad. In fact, in a high interest rate environment, the blended interest and principal repayments become necessary because the interest costs on their own would be prohibitively high.

The interest rate along with the size of your outstanding balance is what determines how much interest you will pay. If you look at the cumulative interest paid, in the first scenario with 8% interest, Mom & Pop ended up paying $580,339, but with the lower rate of 4%, their total interest over the lifetime of the mortgage was only $260,127. This much of a difference in interest payment looks like it presents a significant opportunity, but the interest rate is outside of your control. How can you create these same kinds of savings when you can't change the interest rate?

PREPAYMENTS ARE YOUR GREATEST WEAPON

You can choose a mortgage with a prepayment privilege and use some of the free cash flow you created with your big decisions and budget decisions to make accelerated principal repayments. When you do so, you save in two ways.

First, you save money on the interest costs, which would have otherwise gone out the window if you stayed within the normal amortization period. Ironically, even in a low interest rate environment, you end up paying less over the lifetime of the mortgage.

Second, you save time. By saving time you've bought yourself extra years in which you can use the money in other ways, like saving for retirement. The biggest trap people fall into is that they aren't able to consistently save a large enough percentage of their income to fund their retirement. Once the mortgage is paid, a significant percentage of your income opens up and becomes available to invest.

So you've learned that the amount of payment, interest rate, and length of the mortgage are intrinsically related, but to get ahead you need the ability to step outside of the amortization schedule. You do so by making direct principal repayments.

Now, the banks do provide loans with shorter amortization periods such as ten or fifteen years, but people can be hesitant to choose them because the payment is so much higher. And life happens. No one wants to be locked in to a high payment and then have a bad month and not be able to make it. Instead, what if you took matters into your own hands and structured the payments so that your minimum payment was within your ability to handle ever month, but that you also gave yourself the ability to prepay your mortgage, ultimately freeing up more time to save for retirement and do other things with that money.

How much should you prepay?

If you go through the simple budget system, you can see pretty easily from a needs-based perspective how much money has to be spent every month. You can also see how much free cash flow you have available to accelerate your goals. If you've also looked at your big decisions and budget decisions, you will begin to see where the extra money can come from within your budget. The key again is ensuring that whatever you do, it will be sustainable until you are debt-free or have reached your goal.

The biggest benefit to making prepayments on your mortgage is that there is no interest charged on the extra money you put down. How much of a difference can a prepayment on your mortgage make?

Mom & Pop Average

Mom & Pop Average have seen how much their mortgage payment could increase if interest rates went up. They want to be proactive and pay down the $450,000 owing on their home. They are not sure how much they should prepay, so they want to take a look at the effects of putting between 1% and 10% of their gross family income as a prepayment on their mortgage.

MORTGAGE BALANCE $ 450,000 AT A 4% INTEREST RATE	
Annual family income	$ 86,932.00
Gross monthly income	$ 7,244.33
Mortgage payment	$ 2,367.09

% OF GROSS FAMILY INCOME	EXTRA MONTHLY PAYMENT	COMBINED PAYMENT	TOTAL INTEREST	LENGTH OF MORTGAGE
0%	$ 0	$ 2,367.09	$ 260,127	25 yrs
1%	$ 72.44	$ 2,439.53	$ 245,634	23 yrs, 10 mths
2%	$ 144.89	$ 2,511.98	$ 232,736	22 yrs, 8 mths
3%	$ 217.33	$ 2,584.42	$ 221,181	21 yrs, 8 mths
4%	$ 289.78	$ 2,656.87	$ 210,758	20 yrs, 9 mths
5%	$ 362.22	$ 2,729.31	$ 201,309	19 yrs, 11 mths
6%	$ 434.66	$ 2,801.75	$ 192,698	19 yrs, 2 mths
7%	$ 507.11	$ 2,874.20	$ 184,815	18 yrs, 5 mths
8%	$ 579.55	$ 2,946.64	$ 177,570	17 yrs, 9 mths
9%	$ 651.99	$ 3,019.08	$ 170,888	17 yrs, 2 mths
10%	$ 724.44	$ 3,091.53	$ 164,703	16 yrs, 7 mths

This means that if Mom & Pop Average can find an extra 10% of the income they used to qualify, they could save $95,424 and over eight years time off of their mortgage.

They can see right away that the length of their mortgage decreases as the percentage of income they use to prepay goes up. This example is in a low interest rate scenario, where Mom & Pop Average will see the lowest amount of benefit.

For comparison's sake, instead of buying their house now, let's say that Mom & Pop Average are going to buy that same house for $450,000 at a later point, when interest rates are at 8%. Their income has increased, enabling them to qualify for this home. Again, they want to see the effects of putting an additional 1% to 10% of the gross family income that was used to qualify for the home onto their mortgage as a prepayment.

MORTGAGE BALANCE $ 450,000 AT AN 8% INTEREST RATE	
Annual family income	$ 117,429.00
Gross monthly income	$ 9,785.75
Mortgage payment	$ 3,434.46

% OF GROSS FAMILY INCOME	EXTRA MONTHLY PAYMENT	COMBINED PAYMENT	TOTAL INTEREST	LENGTH OF MORTGAGE
0%	$ 0	$ 3,434.46	$ 580,339	25 yrs
1%	$ 97.86	$ 3,532.32	$ 525,234	23 yrs, 1 mth
2%	$ 195.71	$ 3,630.17	$ 481,003	21 yrs, 5 mths
3%	$ 293.57	$ 3,728.03	$ 444,482	20 yrs

% OF GROSS FAMILY INCOME	EXTRA MONTHLY PAYMENT	COMBINED PAYMENT	TOTAL INTEREST	LENGTH OF MORTGAGE
4%	$ 391.43	$ 3,825.89	$ 413,686	18 yrs, 10 mths
5%	$ 489.29	$ 3,923.75	$ 387,280	17 yrs, 10 mths
6%	$ 587.14	$ 4,021.60	$ 364,336	16 yrs, 11 mths
7%	$ 685.00	$ 4,119.46	$ 344,172	16 yrs, 1 mth
8%	$ 782.86	$ 4,217.32	$ 326,287	15 yrs, 5 mths
9%	$ 880.72	$ 4,315.18	$ 310,297	14 yrs, 9 mths
10%	$ 978.57	$ 4,413.03	$ 295,902	14 yrs, 1 mth

In this scenario, the only thing that has changed is the interest rate. However, with 8% instead of 4% on their mortgage, the extra prepayment of 10% would save them $284,437 and nearly eleven years of time. Now if that money were invested and allowed to grow, it could become a nice little nest egg!

Mr. Metro: Big Mortgages Amplify the Results

Now, Mom and Pop Average's $450,000 mortgage nicely represents the average price for housing, but what about those who take out a mortgage above the average? Depending on where you live, a $1,000,000 mortgage can be common in some of the more metropolitan areas.

Mr. Metro decided to test his savings in the same way as Mom & Pop Average (at 4% and 8%) and was shocked to see the results!

MORGAGE BALANCE OUTSTANDING: $ 1,000,000 AT A 4% INTEREST RATE	
Annual family income	$ 180,925.00
Gross monthly income	$ 15,077.08
Mortgage payment	$ 5,260.20

% OF GROSS FAMILY INCOME	EXTRA MONTHLY PAYMENT	COMBINED PAYMENT	TOTAL INTEREST	LENGTH OF MORTGAGE
0%	$ 0	$ 5,260.20	$ 578,061	25 yrs
1%	$ 150.77	$ 5,410.97	$ 547,783	23 yrs, 10 mths
2%	$ 301.54	$ 5,561.74	$ 520,655	22 yrs, 10 mths
3%	$ 452.31	$ 5,712.51	$ 496,194	21 yrs, 10 mths
4%	$ 603.08	$ 5,863.28	$ 474,014	21 yrs
5%	$ 753.85	$ 6,014.05	$ 453,802	20 yrs, 2 mths
6%	$ 904.62	$ 6,164.82	$ 435,300	19 yrs, 5 mths
7%	$ 1,055.40	$ 6,315.60	$ 418,294	18 yrs, 9 mths
8%	$ 1,206.17	$ 6,466.37	$ 402,607	18 yrs, 1 mth
9%	$ 1,356.94	$ 6,617.14	$ 388,087	17 yrs, 6 mths
10%	$ 1,507.71	$ 6,767.91	$ 374,606	17 yrs

By making an extra 10% prepayment, Mr. Metro could save himself $203,455 and eight years' time. That seems like a pretty nice amount of savings. Until he looked at what it would be at 8%.

MORTGAGE BALANCE OUTSTANDING: $ 1,000,000 AT AN 8% INTEREST RATE	
Annual family income	$ 248,694.00
Gross monthly income	$ 20,724.50
Mortgage payment	$ 7,632.13

% OF GROSS FAMILY INCOME	EXTRA MONTHLY PAYMENT	COMBINED PAYMENT	TOTAL INTEREST	LENGTH OF MORTGAGE
0%	$ 0	$ 7,632.13	$ 1,289,643	25 yrs
1%	$ 207.25	$ 7,839.38	$ 1,172,331	23 yrs, 2 mths
2%	$ 414.49	$ 8,046.62	$ 1,077,313	21 yrs, 7 mths
3%	$ 621.74	$ 8,253.87	$ 998,321	20 yrs, 3 mths
4%	$ 828.98	$ 8,461.11	$ 931,343	19 yrs, 1 mth
5%	$ 1,036.23	$ 8,668.36	$ 873,650	18 yrs, 1 mth
6%	$ 1,243.47	$ 8,875.60	$ 823,324	17 yrs, 2 mths
7%	$ 1,450.72	$ 9,082.85	$ 778,952	16 yrs, 4 mths
8%	$ 1,657.96	$ 9,290.09	$ 739,485	15 yrs, 8 mths
9%	$ 1,865.21	$ 9,497.34	$ 704,105	15 yrs
10%	$ 2,072.45	$ 9,704.58	$ 672,183	14 yrs, 5 mths

That's a total savings of $617,460 and nearly eleven years of time. However, Mr. Metro may not have the full 10% of his gross income to use because after all his deductions, he needs to have enough left to maintain his lifestyle. This can be modified by the other big decisions and budget decisions he makes.

Prepayments are your greatest weapon. Not only do you save time but you also save money in terms of the total amount you are putting into your mortgage. By stepping outside of your amortization schedule, the amount you save is the interest costs you would have otherwise paid. Interestingly, the trend of increasing the frequency of your payments, from monthly to biweekly, works because it follows the same theme. Those more frequent payments turn into a small prepayment each year, which enables you to save both time and money on your mortgage.

Where do you get your prepayment money?

If you are thinking of buying a new home, this is the ideal time to take a look at your simple budget, big decisions, and budget decisions to ensure that you can maintain the lifestyle you want on the budget you have. This process is all about trade-offs, and you will need to determine what is most important to you. If having a big house tops the list, then you may have to compromise on location, carpool to save costs, or take public transit. Make decisions that factor in affordability and give you control over what percentage of your income you apply to housing.

HOW MUCH IS YOUR HOUSING REALLY COSTING YOU?

This bring us to a very important point. Housing is important—in fact, it's essential—but there is such a thing as paying too much for your home.

In our example above, when Mr. Metro's $1,000,000 mortgage was at a constant 4% interest rate, he found himself making interest payments of $578,061 on a $1,000,000 mortgage. As interest rates increased, so did the multiplier. At a constant 8% interest rate, he had paid for his mortgage twice over, with $1,289,643 going toward interest!

The interest rate plays a large role in the total cost of your mortgage. The higher the interest rate, the more the real cost of your home increases, as a result making a more powerful and compelling argument for principal prepayments. These higher rates are when prepayments become crucial—the higher the interest rate, the more time and money you can save with your prepayments! The bottom line is that if you choose to do nothing, the choice will be made for you, and you could end up paying thousands more on a house that is already expensive.

Now which would you rather have: a mortgage that lasts twenty-five years or a mortgage that is done in much less time and that costs you less? What would it mean for your future if you were able to redirect the money that was otherwise going to your lender into your own personal savings for retirement? This puts you in the driver's seat and lets you control how quickly you choose to pay off your mortgage. You no longer have to take what the bank tells you to and pay for twenty-five years. You set your own schedule and use all of the extra money as you see fit.

But it doesn't stop there. By looking at your mortgage this way, in addition to saving money on interest costs, you've bought yourself extra time. Your opportunity cost is your freedom. When the mortgage payment is gone, you are able to put all your energy into other pursuits. A mortgage that is paid off significantly ahead of schedule will give you a significant amount of freedom. Which brings us to two very important questions: How important is that extra time to you? How could your life change if you took the money that had been going toward your mortgage and used it in whatever way you saw fit because you'd bought and paid for your own freedom: spending the remainder of your life mortgage-free?

five

THE DEBT-FREE RETIREMENT

FUNDED BY SAVED INTEREST AND TIME

Retirement is a big, beautiful, and completely terrifying proposition. It requires a significant amount of savings to go into it prepared. We all hope for a good, long healthy life, but funding thirty-plus years of retirement is no small undertaking, especially if you are part of the 68% of the labour force who doesn't have a registered pension plan.[66] A long, unhealthy retirement is even more frightening, as the costs for personal care can add up quickly. I've seen far too many adult children think they would inherit the million-dollar family home only to see it sold and the money spent on care costs while the elderly parents are still living. Some of these concerns can be alleviated with proper planning or the use of insurance products like long-term care insurance, which allows the living beneficiaries access to a pool of cash they have purchased in the event of needing different levels of care. This takes the burden off of the loved ones, who may otherwise feel obligated to spend increasing amounts of time and money caring for their ailing parents.

THE TIME TRAP

We know that we need to save for our retirement. It seems so far off, though, that it's easy for us to kick the can farther down the road and put off what we should be doing today for tomorrow. And who can blame us? If we go on to post-secondary education, pay off our consumer debts and student loans, save for a down payment, and then purchase a home in our forties with the standard twenty-five-year amortization period, we'll probably end up paying off the house as we retire, which has given us little to no room for substantial savings. This point is hammered home when we see that the average Canadian household is saving only 4% of their income.[67]

But therein lies the problem. One of the biggest worries on people's minds as they step into our financial planning office for the first time is if they will have enough to retire. Unfortunately, they usually come to us with only a few years (or months!) remaining before retirement. Your retirement planning is far too big and important to leave until the last minute.

Planning for retirement is something that we need to take far more seriously, and with a sense of urgency. What we do today determines our quality of life for the rest of our lives. This is especially true for those who don't have a pension. For those who do, there is still no guarantee that you will stay with that company permanently. Workopolis reported that between 1990 and 2000, 55% to 60% of people stayed in the same job for over four years and only 16% stayed in their job for under two years. But the statistics from 2000 to 2014 told a different story, with 51% now staying in their jobs for less than two years and only 30% holding one job for more than four years.[68] This means that more than ever the responsibility lies on our shoulders. Pensions can change, the level of government benefits can change, and with inflation and the cost of living increasing ever year, you will need a substantial amount of money saved.

Think of it this way: If you start working at age twenty and retire at age sixty-five, you will have had forty-five years in the labour force. If you then live to age one hundred, you will need to fund thirty-five years of retirement. If you went to post-secondary education and began your career later, your working career could be just as long as your retirement! Financial planners used to use age ninety as the lifespan for planning purposes, but with so many Canadians living longer, you don't want to find yourself on the wrong side of a statistic at a time in your life when you can't make any more money and may need to pay for care costs. We now plan to age one hundred to make sure that your retirement is properly funded.

How much do we need to save? Traditional wisdom tells us that we should be saving 10% of our income. If it's done consistently over a lifetime, this is a good number. The trouble is that not everyone will have started at the beginning of their career. Depending on when you begin saving, your financial planner can show you how much you will have saved and how closely that lines up with your projected lifestyle expenditures. Armed with that information, you will then be able to see how much you need to save to reach your ultimate goal. However, due to lifestyle choices, most people are not able to save 10% or more every year. This is why creating a debt-free lifestyle is so important. The years are flying by, so this savings needs to be a part of our regular budget. The lifestyle choices we make are so important because more than any other factor they will determine how successful we will be at saving, which ultimately determines if we will go into our retirement prepared.

Consistent saving over time is essential

The time to begin saving for your retirement is now. I can say that with confidence because the younger you are, the better. You can save a smaller amount over a longer period of time and still come out ahead because the compounding of your investments works like magic. But this compounding needs to be done over a long period of time to realize the maximum benefit.

As I mentioned earlier, saving for retirement is something that Cam and I have done all along the way. This is extremely important. Don't ever let other goals take you away from this one because every day you are a step closer to it and that is time you can't get back. Your financial planner can help you determine how much you should be putting toward your retirement and how much should be focused on your other goals. Even before we began our debt repayment journey, Cam and I were each putting away $50 per month into our RRSPs. I know it sounds like a pittance. Being a financial planner, I also know that $100 per month from our mid-twenties to age sixty-five would only work out to be $118,196 with a 4% rate of return, or $349,100 with an 8% rate of return. But I was okay with this action because of one thing: our timeline.

Cameron and I were twenty-five years old when we began our journey. We made sure that we were making choices that would be workable for our primary goal of debt freedom and secondary goal of a comfortable retirement. We didn't bite off more than we could chew and we bought a property that we could comfortably afford. The prepayment strategy favours the young because not only will we have a base level of consistent retirement savings throughout the years, but once our mortgage is paid, we will have the rest of our careers to save.

On the other hand, in my role as a financial planner, one of the motivations behind this book is that I've met more fifty-year-olds who still have a twenty-five-year mortgage than I'd care to mention. More often than not, they made choices that caused them to live outside of their means and they have found themselves having to refinance. Refinancing may seem like a good idea at the time, but payments are kept low by re-extending the time to pay, which increases the total cost of the mortgage. Now, as the years have gone by, they find themselves wanting to retire in the next ten or fifteen years but are not sure how they can. Their goal of a comfortable retirement now appears to be conflicting with their goal to be debt-free.

What if you are reading this book later in life and it looks like you will still have debt during retirement? Should you shore up your retirement savings or try to reduce as much of your debt as possible before you retire?

It comes down to five factors: the time to your retirement, the percentage of your income that you can save, the amount you have accumulated to date, the size of your outstanding debts, and, most importantly, the amount you will need each month during your retirement to live comfortably.

As we saw with Mom & Pop Average and Mr. Metro, the amount of time saved on their mortgage is directly related to the percentage they will be able to prepay. They need to factor in the amount of savings they could amass to their retirement age. Mr. Metro is facing the very real scenario of going into retirement with a mortgage; with limited time left, he needs to be able to decide if it is more important for him to save extra money or try to go into retirement debt-free. One of the big factors in the decision-making process will be his retirement budget and the amount he has already put aside.

He should ask himself the following questions:

- How much time do I have until I want to retire?
- How much money do I have saved to date, including pension(s), government benefits like Canada Pension Plan (CPP), Old Age Security (OAS) and personal savings?
- How much do I owe: what are the monthly costs for my debt and how much longer will I have them?
- How much more do I need to maintain my lifestyle?

UNDERSTANDING A NEEDS-BASED RETIREMENT

It should come as no surprise that I recommend doing a retirement budget the same way as the simple budget. A needs-based budget speaks to people. It lets them see their actual cost of living in dollar terms that are easy to understand.

I prefer this over rules of thumb such as "use 75% of your pre-retirement income." In my mind, this takes the flexibility out of the equation. People don't really connect with what that means on a lifestyle level. All they hear is that they need to spend 25% less than what they're spending now—and they could already be feeling like they can barely make ends meet as it is.

Retirement is not a static event—it is fluid. It will change, and your expenses will change as you go through it. People usually spend more in their early years as they check items off the bucket list. Then, spending will usually normalize as people get into a daily routine and focus on the more meaningful things in life: such as spending time with family and friends. Finally, unfortunately costs can go up again if health takes a turn for the worst in the later retirement years.[69] The simple retirement budget can help to establish a baseline.

A financial planner can then determine the amount of after-tax income you will need at a minimum during retirement. He or she will include factors like investment growth, the loss of purchasing power through inflation, and taxes. But for all the extras financial planners throw in to try to give you a more comprehensive picture, it all comes down to you.

How does your needs-based retirement budget look when you also have to make a mortgage payment? Can you sustain it or are you barely getting by? Maybe you've saved well or maybe a generous pension makes you feel like this won't be a problem. But you may feel that a mortgage payment—or even rent, for that matter—can make the amount you need to save feel more unattainable. In fact, you may begin to see how you will have to save a lot more under those circumstances.

RENTING

Prepaying your home, or even buying a home altogether, may not be right for everyone. Even though I am convinced that there are some significant advantages to buying a home and going into retirement debt-free, I understand that there are circumstances when other decisions would be more beneficial.

Whatever the reason, according to the Federation of Canadian Municipalities, one-third of Canadians are renters.[70]

Renting and investing the difference has become a popular concept. While some people struggle to qualify for a home, others simply don't want to be bothered with home ownership due to their own lifestyle decisions. For those who have committed to the program of renting and investing the difference, they will see how quickly their savings can grow. This is a wonderful thing, but it is good to keep in mind that if RRSPs were used for tax deferral, every dollar that comes out is 100% taxable. This means that the person who needs to rent during retirement will need to save a considerable amount more than the person who has already paid for, or is just finishing paying for, their home. It may also mean that that individual will need to take more out of their savings each year than the person living rent-free, which can increase the amount of tax owing each year since tax rates in Canada increase with our income. Depending on the income level and amount that needs to be withdrawn, factors such as the clawback of Old Age Security may come in play. In addition, rent can increase every year, along with the cost of living, and all these factors can cause a significant strain on savings.

According to the CMHC's Rental Market Report for spring 2015, the average monthly rent for a two-bedroom apartment was $949 across Canada's thirty-five major centres. The highest average monthly rent was found in Vancouver, at $1,345.

While interest rate increases are the biggest threat to a home-owner, rent increases can have a similar impact on a tenant. Each year the landlord is allowed to increase rent by a standard amount that is published by the applicable province, unless the tenant and landlord have their own agreement in writing. In British Columbia, that rate increase in 2015 was 2.5%.[71] Over the last ten-year period, the lowest amount of the increase was 2.2% in 2014 and the highest was 4.6% in 2004.

If the average Canadian rent were to increase 2.5% every year for the next twenty-five years—which is the standard length of a mortgage—at the end of the time period when the homeowner's mortgage is paid off, the renter may have gone from paying $949 per month to $1,759. Unless there are corresponding cost of living increases in the wages we get paid, the percentage of our budget going toward housing costs will creep upward. This means that by retirement, the advantage between renting and owning could be eaten up by increasing rental costs. I could now find myself going into my golden years with rent higher than ever at a point in my life where my income is the lowest it has ever been.

A person who owns a home during retirement will need to save considerably less for their retirement, as only the upkeep, utilities, property tax, and other ongoing costs of the shelter will need to be included in their budget. Those who rent will have to have saved enough money to continue to pay their rent during their golden years. So the big question becomes—if you rent and save the difference, are you saving for your retirement or have you just saved enough to continue to cover your rent?

Finding affordable rent can be a problem

According to the CMHC's spring 2015 rental report, the vacancy rate across Canada as measured by the thirty-five major centres was an average of 2.9% in April 2015. In Vancouver, the vacancy rate in that same time period was only 1.4%.

In years to come, it may become less profitable for independent landlords to hold certain types of rental units. As buildings get older, landlords who are part of condominium, apartment, or townhouse complexes may find that fees or special levies to do maintenance and repairs are increasing. There will be a point where, with the limit to rent increases, costs become prohibitively high and these rental properties become less profitable. If so, those who have purchased properties for the sake of cash flow may direct their attention to other projects with a higher return or freestanding dwellings where the maintenance costs can be more easily controlled.

MISSING GROWTH

Would you say that real estate prices have been stagnant over the past few years? According to the Canadian Real Estate Association (CREA), housing prices as tracked by the MLS Home Price Index (HPI) rose 6.9% across Canada from September 2014 to September 2015.[72] When we look at the change of value in the housing market today, one of the reasons that it is so hard to get into a new property is because the value of a home has increased considerably.

According to the No Vacancy Report by the Federation of Canadian Municipalities, the average price to buy a new home in Canada nearly doubled, from $234,387 in 2001 to $454,154 in 2010. In fact, CREA has a national aggregate Home Price Index Benchmark that showed housing price increases of 26.18% in the past five years.[73] The percentage change varied widely across Canada, with areas like Greater Toronto, Greater Vancouver, the Lower Mainland, and Calgary showing the largest percentages of growth. This argument is more for those who are comparing renting with buying a home because the increase in the home as an asset is an important piece that renters miss out on. In the interest of diversification, real estate is a different asset class than your investments in stocks or bonds, which means performance won't be correlated and there can be significant advantages to owing both. The difference between owning and renting may simply be the ability to save for a down payment, which can be made a reality with the cash flow that becomes available from making proper lifestyle choices.

RETIRING WITH DEBT

We know that the prepayment strategy is most beneficial for people who take out their mortgage while they are young. Once the mortgage is paid, they have a long stretch of time before retirement in which they can now save a much larger percentage of their income and head into retirement prepared. But what about the person who is closer to retirement and does not yet have enough saved? Should he or she focus on prepayment or on saving?

The retirement budget was the first step in the decision process. If you need more money saved and your time horizon is short, you are better off putting your money into savings. In addition, if you are a good way into your mortgage already, you may want to take a close look at what Mom & Pop Average just realized.

Mom & Pop Average: The timing of prepayments matter

Let's go back to Mom & Pop Average and their $450,000 mortgage, using all the same parameters we defined earlier. Our happy family now finds themselves in a scenario where interest rates are increasing modestly. As we've seen, rising interest rates means that the total cost to pay off the mortgage will increase.

BALANCE: $ 450,000		WITHOUT PREPAYMENTS		
YEAR	INTEREST RATE	PAYMENT	BALANCE OUTSTANDING	TOTAL INTEREST
1–5	4%	$ 2,367.09	$ 391,743	
6–10	4%	$ 2,367.09	$ 320,727	
11–15	5%	$ 2,527.73	$ 238,882	
16–20	6%	$ 2,643.25	$ 136,966	
21–25	6%	$ 2,643.25	$ 0	$ 302,905

With interest rates increasing modestly as Mom & Pop Average pay down their mortgage over twenty-five years, they only saw a modest increase in the amount of their mortgage payment during its lifetime. However, because of the increase in interest rates on the balance outstanding, they paid total interest of $302,905 on top of the $450,000, making the total cost of their home $752,905.

Now let's say that Mom & Pop Average worked out the simple budget system and start making a prepayment of 5% of the gross family income they qualified with. That 5% works out to an extra $362.22 a month. But then, after the first ten years of the mortgage, circumstances change and they do not make any more prepayments but continue with the original schedule. Was it worth it to make the prepayments in the early years?

BALANCE: $450,000		ADDITIONAL PREPAYMENT OF $362.22 PER MONTH FOR THE *FIRST* 10 YEARS		
YEAR	INTEREST RATE	PAYMENT	BALANCE OUTSTANDING	TOTAL INTEREST
1–5	4%	$ 2,729.31	$ 367,748	
6–10	4%	$ 2,729.31	$ 267,483	
11–15	5%	$ 2,527.73	$ 170,725	
16–20	6%	$ 2,643.25	$ 45,369	
21–25	6%	$ 2,643.25	$ 0	$ 235,301

In addition, the mortgage is paid off three and a half years ahead of schedule.

In real life, if Mom & Pop Average have equity and change lenders or refinance, the lenders may offer them a lower payment amount to extend the payment period back to the full twenty-five years instead of sticking to the original schedule, shortened by the prepayments. If managing the monthly payment amount is the primary concern, then Mom & Pop Average could chose to extend the payment schedule, and their payments would be $2,108.10 at 5% between Years 11–15 and $2,204.43 at 6% between Years 16–25. The total interest they would pay in this schedule would be $268,536.

In the following scenario, Mom & Pop Average were not able to make prepayments early on. They do not have any extra money until the last ten years of the mortgage. They make the exact same amount of prepayments as they did in the previous scenario but with significantly different results.

BALANCE: $ 450,000		ADDITIONAL PREPAYMENT OF $362.22 PER MONTH FOR THE *LAST* 10 YEARS		
YEAR	INTEREST RATE	PAYMENT	BALANCE OUTSTANDING	TOTAL INTEREST
1–5	4%	$ 2,367.09	$ 391,743	
6–10	4%	$ 2,367.09	$ 320,727	
11–15	5%	$ 2,527.73	$ 238,882	
16–20	6%	$ 3,005.47	$ 111,742	
21–25	6%	$ 3,005.47	$ 0	$ 289,807

The mortgage would end a year and a half ahead of schedule.

By putting it all together, Mom and Pop Average can see that the additional $362.22 a month saved them a large amount of money when it was applied early on in the mortgage and much, much less when that same additional amount was applied during the last ten years. In addition, they had made more payments in total because the increasing interest rate had bumped up their monthly payment amount when the terms renewed every five years.

AMOUNT OF THE MORTGAGE: $ 450,000				
	TOTAL PAYMENTS	TOTAL INTEREST	INTEREST SAVED	TIME SAVED
Without prepayment	$ 752,905	$ 302,905	$ 0	none
Prepayment in first 10 years	$ 685,301	$ 235,301	$ 67,604	3 yrs, 6 mths
Prepayment in last 10 years	$ 739,807	$ 289,807	$ 13,098	1 yr, 6 mths

How can this be? Because Mom & Pop Average were able to decrease the outstanding mortgage balance during the early years, the total interest over the lifetime of the mortgage was reduced, lowering their total cost. In the later years of the mortgage, the interest had already mostly been paid, so the only variable that can change is the time they have remaining. In this case, they could not save much money on interest payments, and the time frame could only be shortened by so much.

Mr. Metro's prepayment dilemma

Things compound for Mr. Metro when he finds himself in a scenario in which interest rates are higher but decreasing.

This helps him to feel less concerned about his payments increasing, but higher interest early on can still put him in the danger zone of paying too much for his home. This problem is compounded by the size of his mortgage. In this scenario, the prepayments early on make a significant difference.

BALANCE: $1,000,000		WITHOUT ANY PREPAYMENTS		
YEAR	INTEREST RATE	PAYMENT	BALANCE OUTSTANDING	TOTAL INTEREST
1–5	12%	$ 10,319.00	$ 954,601	
6–10	12%	$ 10,319.00	$ 873,299	
11–15	10%	$ 9,276.79	$ 707,970	
16–20	8%	$ 8,541.01	$ 422,527	
21–25	8%	$ 8,541.01	$ 0	$ 1,819,810

It is important to note once again that Mr. Metro's prepayment is significantly higher because it is a percentage of the gross family income that he would need to qualify for a mortgage at 12%. Mr. Metro's income would need to be a whopping $387,126 a year to qualify with the expenses we had previously outlined under the gross debt service ratio rules, or $325,462 using the total debt service ratio rules. Compare this with the gross income of $213,681 using the gross debt service ratio or $180,925 using the total debt service ratio that he would need to be eligible for that exact same $1,000,000 mortgage at a 4% interest rate. What an amazing influence the interest rate has on the amount he can qualify for. This is a good thing for first-time homebuyers to keep in mind.

With 5% of Mr. Metro's income as a prepayment based on the total debt service ratio, he would be looking to add $1,356.09 a month to his already high payment. Keep in mind that with the high salary that would be needed to qualify for the $1,000,000 mortgage at 12%, his before-tax monthly income in this example would be $27,122. If we changed nothing in this scenario but the first ten years, it would look like this:

BALANCE: $1,000,000		ADDITIONAL PREPAYMENT OF $1,356.09 PER MONTH FOR THE *FIRST* 10 YEARS		
YEAR	INTEREST RATE	PAYMENT	BALANCE OUTSTANDING	TOTAL INTEREST
1–5	12%	$ 11,675.09	$ 844,704	
6–10	12%	$ 11,675.09	$ 566,594	
11–15	10%	$ 9,276.79	$ 208,379	
16–20	8%	$ 8,541.01	$ 0	
21–25	8%	$ 0.00	$ 0	$ 1,185,435

Mr. Metro's prepayments would free up seven years and nine months. If, however, during the last ten years he wanted to make the payments lower and take the rest of the twenty-five years in the amortization schedule to pay, his balance outstanding of $208,379 at the end of Year 15 would mean that even with an 8% interest rate, he could drop his monthly payments all the way down to $2,513.90 to help him manage his cash flow during retirement.

The following scenario shows the results of Mr. Metro's prepayments at the end of the mortgage:

BALANCE: $1,000,000		ADDITIONAL PREPAYMENT OF $1,356.09 PER MONTH FOR THE *LAST* 10 YEARS		
YEAR	INTEREST RATE	PAYMENT	BALANCE OUTSTANDING	TOTAL INTEREST
1–5	12%	$ 10,319.00	$ 954,601	
6–10	12%	$ 10,319.00	$ 873,299	
11–15	10%	$ 9,276.79	$ 707,970	
16–20	8%	$ 9,897.10	$ 323,223	
21–25	8%	$ 9,897.10	$ 0	$ 1,753,644

These prepayments in the last ten years only freed up one year and eleven months' time.

By putting it all together for Mr. Metro, we can see the effects of prepayments on a large mortgage in a high but decreasing interest rate environment:

AMOUNT OF THE MORTGAGE: $1,000,000				
	TOTAL PAYMENTS	TOTAL INTEREST	INTEREST SAVED	TIME SAVED
Without prepayment	$ 2,819,810	$ 1,819,810	$ 0	none
Prepayment in first 10 years	$ 2,185,435	$ 1,185,435	$ 634,375	7 yrs, 9 mths
Prepayment in last 10 years	$ 2,753,644	$ 1,753,644	$ 66,166	1 yr, 11 mths

By making a prepayment of 5% of his qualifying income, in the first ten years of the mortgage, not only was less money paid out of pocket but also $634,375 was saved in interest costs. The higher interest rates amplified the effects of the prepayments made early on in the amortization schedule. If that weren't enough, Mr. Metro would have bought himself extra time to save all of this money for other things, like his retirement. Where would you like your money to go? To interest paid to the bank or into your own pocket, where it can earn interest and grow on your behalf?

Closed mortgages and prepayments

Closed mortgages have a specified amount that you can prepay each year: the maximum is usually 20% of the original mortgage balance. As the balance of your mortgage whittles down, depending on the percentage of prepayments you make, you may want to switch a closed mortgage for an open one in the last few years.

Cam and I are a bit unusual because when we began, before my theories were tested, all we knew is that we wanted to be debt-free more than we wanted anything else. We were young and we knew that if we achieved that goal quickly we would have plenty of time to save before our retirement. Our process was to follow the simple budget every week and apply every dollar that we didn't need to use toward our debt. We structured our mortgage as an open line of credit because we didn't want to worry about being penalized for overpayments. However, in hindsight, these vehicles can have interest compound more frequently, which raises the total interest cost. They are also immediately subject to interest rate increases, so can be riskier to your budget if it is already tight. Because our outstanding balance was low and interest rates were low, we were comfortable with this structure. However, most of my clients had traditional mortgages, and I wanted to find a way to replicate what we were able to do without being reliant on low interest rates. What I found was that the method of using prepayments against the mortgage early on was even more effective in a higher interest rate environment and led to even greater savings. In a high interest rate environment, you would not want an open line of credit unless the mortgage was almost done and the balance was very small because the interest cost can become prohibitively high. The blend of principal and interest in a mortgage can actually be a huge advantage in a high interest rate environment if you chose to prepay; but if you don't, it can be disastrous for your total costs paid.

Prepayment timing is everything

As I've mentioned, timing is important. Before we even begin to look at comparing making an investment with a prepayment on our mortgage, we need to ask ourselves, When we will be able to do so? More specifically, how far into the amortization schedule are we? While the prepayment option can deliver great results during the first portion of the mortgage when interest makes up the bulk of your payment, this advantage starts to diminish as the principal becomes a bigger percentage of each payment. At this point, you will save time but not as much money in interest.

Think back to the amortization schedule structure that we looked at earlier. There was lots of interest and less principal repayments in the early years and less interest and more principal repaid later on. This tells us that the timing of our mortgage prepayments makes a big difference. If you think of your mortgage as a cost in terms of total interest paid, prepayments made earlier on will have a significantly greater effect on the total interest costs over the lifetime of the mortgage and on the time that you will free up to pursue other goals. Prepayments made later on in the mortgage will still have a positive effect, but the overall benefit will be lessened because you've already paid out a large percentage of the interest costs up front.

The reality is, you pay the most in interest during the first portion of the mortgage, so let the amortization schedule be your guide.

The right answer for you will be found in a combination of factors:

- the amount of money you have available to either prepay or put in an investment
- the length of time before you will stop working and need to begin withdrawing the money
- the amount of money you'll have from other sources during retirement

Are prepayments right for you?
After the first year of using the simple budget system, you will have a reasonable idea of the percentage you will be able

to commit, but even then it will vary from year to year. We've had years where it was a bit higher, and we've had years where it was far lower than we expected because life just keeps on happening. The whole point of the simple budget system is to give you some guidelines for your thought process and to point you in the right direction.

The Debt-Free Lifestyle is about creating a lifestyle—one that you will not only enjoy but can also sustain over the long-term. If you have properly addressed the big decisions and budget decisions and have made decisions based on an affordability ratio that works for you, it should be no trouble to continue with this lifestyle after the mortgage is paid. You can then perhaps loosen up the spending or give yourself more fun money in your simple budget, but ultimately you should have close to the whole amount that you were pre-paying to invest for your retirement.

Cam and I have discussed that once our mortgage is paid, we will give ourselves a bit more fun money to reflect our new cash flow and because our earnings are a bit higher than when we began. But ultimately we will continue our debt-free lifestyle by redirecting the majority of what we were putting toward our home into savings for retirement. In my mind, the biggest thing that we have bought ourselves is freedom. We are free from the worry of what interest rates may do and will have the flexibility to meet challenges as they arise while still having the cash flow to save for our retirement. I want you to experience that freedom too.

six

MORTGAGES AND INVESTMENTS

DO YOU PAY DOWN DEBT OR INVEST?

It's such a widespread concept that it almost sounds like common sense: when interest rates are low, you should invest rather than pay down your debts because you can earn a greater rate of return in the markets over the long run than you can by paying off your debts. There is truth to this, but it's not quite as straightforward as we have been led to believe.

TIMING IS EVERYTHING

We've already demystified one of the first big factors when deciding whether to invest or to pay down your mortgage: the timing of the prepayment. Prepayments made at the beginning of the mortgage will have a significantly greater impact than prepayments made later on. The first part of the decision is clear. If you are beginning your mortgage, you can realize the maximum benefit from prepayment. If you are already toward the end of your mortgage and most of the interest has been paid, that money would be better off invested.

THE SIZE OF YOUR MORTGAGE MATTERS

However, the amount you can save through prepayments is limited to the size of the mortgage balance and the interest rate—both now and in the future. This means that prepayments are more effective on mortgages with a larger balance simply because more cumulative interest will need to be paid. Also, a higher balance is still subject to the amortization schedule, which will keep the outstanding balance high during the first portion of the mortgage, amplifying the effects of a change of interest rates.

YOUR PREPAYMENT AMOUNT MATTERS

Prepayments are beneficial because of their ability to save costs and also create time. However, the amount of money you can save and the time you can create will be directly related to the percentage of your income you consistently apply to this program. That is why *The Debt-Free Lifestyle* system is all about creating a lifestyle that frees up a significant amount of cash flow.

- *The Debt-Free Lifestyle* system helps you determine which lifestyle choices can create the money you need to reach your goals.
- The simple budget shows you how to create free cash flow so you can prepay or save money for the future.
- The simple retirement budget gives you an idea of how much money you will need to accumulate for retirement and should take into account pension plans, government benefits, and other level of savings. You'll want a CFP Professional to help you with this step.

However, the end goal should always be to save enough money to comfortably retire while managing your debt load, paying it off sooner, and ensuring that you don't end up overpaying for your home.

One factor that continually stands out more than any other in this process is that the amount of your income you are able to *consistently* save makes the biggest difference in your ability to go into your retirement prepared. I would go as far to say that this is just as important as the rate of return you earn because it is a factor you can control. If you are completely dependent on high rates of return to fund your retirement and the markets don't cooperate, then you could end up with a retirement plan that is underfunded. Not to mention that you would go through a world of stress because you are relying on a factor you cannot influence.

With a debt-free lifestyle, we are much more concerned with factors within our control, which is why we have to make lifestyle choices that allow for a consistently high level of savings.

For example, if Mom & Pop Average invested 1%, 5%, or 10% of their income when they qualified for their twenty-five-year $450,000 mortgage at 4%, they would get the following results at the end of that twenty-five year period:

% OF GROSS QUALIFYING INCOME	MONTHLY	RATE OF RETURN	
		4%	8%
1%	$ 72.44	$ 37,245	$ 68,896
5%	$ 362.22	$ 186,228	$ 344,480
10%	$ 724.44	$ 372,455	$ 688,960

Money grows money, which is why a smaller amount of savings even at a higher rate of return is still not enough to live on during retirement and a higher amount consistently saved over those same twenty-five years can lead to a much more sufficient nest egg. The question becomes: Do you want to leave it to chance, or are you willing to use *The Debt-Free Lifestyle* system to create an amount of savings you can count on?

THE EFFECTS OF COMPOUND INTEREST

Looking at the amount that Mom & Pop Average can save over time, you might say to yourself, Why should I prepay at all? After all, you've probably been hearing for years that a consistently high rate of return will outperform prepayments at a lower interest rate—and this is true. The effects of compounding interest on interest year over year at a consistently high rate can bake in growth that a low interest rate on a mortgage cannot catch up with. But this misses an important factor: the interest rate on the mortgage will not necessarily stay consistently low over a twenty-five-year period, at least not if history is any indication of the future. Some of us will remember mortgage rates of upward of 20% in the 1980s. Changes to interest rates will impact your mortgage payments, based on the mortgage balance you have outstanding. Depending on when this occurs and how quickly your family income increases, you may find yourself needing the extra cash flow you created with *The Debt-Free Lifestyle* system.

PREPAYMENT COMPARISONS SHOULD USE LONG-TERM AVERAGES TOO

While the financial industry has been really good at looking at average annual rates of return on investments, a flat interest rate is usually used on mortgages for comparison. I have done that too throughout this book to show the pure effects of the amortization schedule and prepayments. But real life is not that straightforward, so in this chapter we'll look at how a rising interest rate scenario could play out in reality.

You'll recall in Chapter 1 we looked at the average five-year residential mortgage rates, as published by the Bank of Canada. Using the bank's list, if we took the interest rate on January 1 from 1995 to 2015, we would have an average rate of 6.67%. If we took a further step back to look at the rates from 1970 to 1990, we would have an average rate of 12.02%.

According to a chart of historical returns compiled by Taxtips.com, for the thirty-six years from December 31, 1979, to December 31, 2015, the S&P/TSX had an average annual return of 8.6% and the S&P 500 American index (in Canadian dollars) had a thirty-six-year average annual return of 12%. Data from the Emerging Markets, again in Canadian dollars, dated back only to December 31, 1987, but for the twenty-eight years from that time to December 31, 2015, the average annual rate of return was 10.7%. However, the same source also showed ten-year rate of return information that told a different story, with the S&P/TSX at 4.4%, the S&P 500 at 9.2%, and the Emerging Markets at 5.7%.[74] This goes to show that the time horizon can mean everything when trying to accurately choose a rate of return for the sake of a projection.

The Financial Planning Standards Council publishes guidelines[75] as to what an appropriate rate of return would be in long-term financial projections. The returns change each year and take into account inflation, fees and the actual performance of equities, and fixed income—which is a more complete picture than simply looking at an index. In 2015, with inflation at 2%, Canadian equities had a rate of return of 6.3% and fixed income had a rate of return of 3.9%. However, most people will have a blend of the two. For an individual with 75% equity, 20% fixed income, and 5% cash, the gross rate of return used for projection purposes is 5.65%. The guidelines also recommend taking into account fees of 1.99% for 2015 and then using the net return in the long-term projection. For an individual with this risk profile, it would be 3.7%. However, for the sake of example, we will use 4% and 8% to take into account the variances that can occur with different time horizons.

While assumptions have their place, they are no substitute for a good old-fashioned annual review that compares what you *thought* would happen to what actually *did* happen, allowing you to adjust your projections accordingly. If these regular reviews are not done, then you could end up being way off the mark if market performance is less than expected. Markets are cyclical, and as much as we would all love to see them go up all the time, there will be times of contraction or recession that we just need to accept as part of our reality and build that into our expectations.

In addition, when we compare investing to prepayments, the interest on your mortgage is a sure thing. There is no risk to prepayments, especially if you know you can exceed the amount earned on your investments due to the size and interest rate of your mortgage. Prepayments when you are locked into a term are a safe way to earn a guaranteed return.

But why not do both? We've learned that every mortgage has a point where prepayments stop becoming beneficial. This means that investing and prepayments actually work together—as long as you know how to determine when to prepay and when to stop prepaying so you can then turn all your efforts toward investing.

FINDING THE BALANCE BETWEEN INVESTING AND PREPAYMENTS

Ironically, the argument most often used for promoting investing, the miracle of compound interest, is the very thing working against you with your debts. It goes like this: given a long enough time horizon, typically the same twenty-five-year period of your mortgage, for comparison's sake, the longer you save, the more you will have because if you don't make withdrawals from your account, each dollar you contribute will grow and multiply.

But when you start saving, you typically don't start with very much. If you open a new RRSP and you earn an 8% net rate of return in the first year on the first $1,000, you've made $80. The compounding for your RRSP really begins to pay off a number of years down the road when you have a larger amount saved.

However, if you're early on in your mortgage, you have the full amount of the debt to service. In fact, you find yourself in the exact opposite position. If you've just taken out a mortgage, your debt is at the highest level it will be. It's not just the performance of that one dollar we need to look at—it's the dollar's ability to decrease your total costs and shorten the lifetime of your mortgage. Every extra dollar you're able to contribute to your principal reduces the total amount of interest you'll pay over the lifetime of the mortgage. That is because interest has a compounding effect too, but instead of working for you, it's working against you. The interest rate you are paying is charged on the whole amount, so the higher the debt, the higher your total interest bill.

With Mom & Pop Average's $450,000 mortgage with a 4% interest rate, their total interest bill in that first year is $17,658. Because of the blend of the amortization schedule, every year this amount will decrease. But in that first year if you try to apply the old adage of investing when interest rates are low, it doesn't look so good: the interest costs at 4% on $450,000 are $17,658, whereas the 8% annual growth on $1,000 is only $80. Now, of course, this isn't the complete picture because it doesn't take into account the whole length of time, but it does bring up a very interesting point.

With every year that passes, your mortgage balance declines and your investments grow. Like a big letter X, they are essentially moving in opposite directions. This is why it is crucial that you do both. The investments make sure that you will be ready for your retirement, and the prepayments will save you money and keep the cost of your home at a reasonable level.

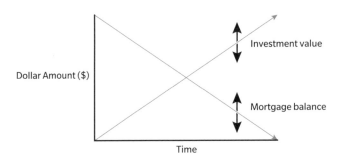

The investment axis can move up or down depending on the rate of return. The amount paid on the mortgage can move up or down depending on the interest rate.

In the early years of your mortgage, you will get the biggest bang for your buck on the interest saved. However, once the balance in your investment accounts starts to exceed the balance on your mortgage, you may want to stop prepaying and turn 100% of your efforts toward investing depending on your average mortgage rate and average rate of return. Even though you get maximum value from prepaying your mortgage early on, because the mortgage balance is decreasing, you need to invest regularly to elevate your savings to ensure you are ready for retirement.

HOW DO YOU BEGIN?

To begin, look at the amount of savings you have to date and look at the balance outstanding on your mortgage. Given the interest rate on your mortgage and the rate of return you expect to achieve, you can see on a dollar basis which action will be better for you at that time. Next, you want to look beyond today at the long-term effects of this action, while also giving consideration to the other factors that could impact the outcome, including the effects of compounding. This can be done by your financial planner by creating different scenarios and comparing the different outcomes. Then, as the years go by you'll want to continue to review and monitor these projections. Think of it like a game of archery: when you have a long time horizon, the target is far away, so the first arrow may hit the outer rim. As the years go by, the target gets closer, until it becomes easy to hit a bull's eye.

However, in reality, changing interest rates and increased mortgage payments may limit your free cash flow and make the decision of when to stop prepaying for you. During the process, you should not stop saving for retirement. Whether it's through employer contributions on your pension at work or from your own efforts, you need to be making consistent savings all the way through. The percentage of income you save, the rate of return you earn, as well as your interest rate and where you are in the amortization schedule will all help determine the best course of action.

APPLY THE OPPORTUNITY COST TESTS

In some cases, if you're too focused on prepayments, you may not end up with enough saved for retirement. If your

CFP Professional runs these tests and the results show that you should be prepaying well beyond the halfway point in your mortgage, a few things may have happened:

- *Your mortgage balance is very high.*
  The benefits of prepayment decrease with the size of your mortgage balance over time. However, some mortgages are just so big that it takes until near the end of the mortgage to ramp up your savings to a comparable level. If this is the case, you may have taken on too much and it may be hurting your ability to save for the future. Your housing costs should never come at the expense of saving enough money for your retirement. If you haven't yet bought a house, your goal should be to create enough cash flow through your lifestyle choices to overcome the high mortgage balance early on and shorten the length of the mortgage. Alternatively, you can save up a large down payment or purchase a home that is less than what you qualify for to achieve the same balance.

- *You're not saving enough to begin with.*
  If this is the case, you may want to look at what you are projected to have saved in total by retirement. Keep in mind that this strategy is an optimization strategy—designed to save you time and interest— but the ultimate goal is to save enough to comfortably

retire. If it doesn't look like you will have enough
to retire, focus on that instead, or use your debt-free
lifestyle to free up additional cash flow and have your
CFP Professional test the scenario again.

The opposite is also true:

- *Your mortgage balance is small.*
  If you have a small balance outstanding on your
  mortgage, you will only save a limited amount of
  interest by prepaying. The effects of compounding
  in your investment portfolio for a long period of
  time may outweigh the benefits of prepayment,
  depending on the time you have left until your
  retirement.

- *You have only a small amount to prepay.*
  The same holds true if you have only a small
  amount to put down on your mortgage each year.
  The small amount may not shorten the amortization
  period enough to make much of a difference in your
  total program, and as a result you may lose out on
  the effects of compounding that you would have
  had if that money had gone into your investments.
  On the other hand, if you can prepay a large percentage, it may shorten the total length of the mortgage
  dramatically—even cut it in half. Even if this is the
  case, you should still be putting money into your

investments along the way so that you don't end up timing the markets and trying to put it all in right before retirement. The amount of income you apply consistently to the program will make all the difference. The time until your retirement and the time you can create with your prepayments will also be determining factors.

THE EFFECTS OF COMPOUNDING ON YOUR INVESTMENTS

If there is a large difference between the average interest rate on your mortgage and your long-term rate of return, then the cumulative effects of compound interest will play a role in your decision.

To run this test, have your CFP Professional line up your mortgage and your investments side by side, but this time, rather than comparing the actual performance year by year, he or she will be comparing the opportunity cost. This is where you compare your projected long-term rate of return to the interest savings you would get from prepaying the mortgage. If you have a long-time horizon, the effects of compounding in the projection can alter the outcomes considerably. So don't forget your annual reviews to temper your best-case scenario with a dose of reality, and your financial planner can adjust your long-term projections accordingly as the years go by.

The length of time your investments are able to compound also matters because this is where the magic of compound interest comes into play. It will do you a limited amount of good if you wait until right before your retirement to stash away a large amount of money. It is best if you are consistently saving for retirement all the way through, giving that money a chance to grow. For this reason, the split between prepayments and investments should be very carefully considered to achieve the ultimate balance.

Once you've looked at the effects of compound interest, have your financial planner test the other variables as well. Will you be putting money into an RRSP and reinvesting your refund? Have that factored into your test. Do you only have a small amount to invest this year and aren't sure if it's big enough to make a difference? Make sure your financial planner tests it. Only a short time left until retirement? That should be tested too.

YOUR RRSP REFUND

If you decide to use an RRSP to invest, the ability to generate a tax refund, depending on the rest of your tax situation, creates an interesting variable and can be a powerful tool. Often when scenarios are run, the RRSP refund is put back into the RRSP, but in reality you can use it to pay down your mortgage. You have the ability to choose where it will serve you best.

The benefit of a refund is dependent on the tax bracket you fall into in a given year, which varies by province. As such, it is much more beneficial for people with higher income than those with lower income. Using the RRSP will allow you to defer paying those taxes to when you make a future withdrawal. If owing tax is a concern for you, it can be beneficial to figure out how much of an RRSP contribution it will take to bring you back to even.

In addition, not every dollar saved should go into RRSPs. Even people with high income will want to have access to a pool of cash that they don't need to pay tax to get at during their retirement, and that is where tax-free savings accounts (TFSAs) and non-registered accounts come in. Due to their flexibility and accessibility, TFSAs play a significant role in long-term planning and should be a part of every Canadian's retirement plan.

USING THE TIME YOU HAVE LEFT

When the comparisons between investments and prepayments are usually done, a twenty-five-year period is used to represent the lifetime of the mortgage. In my mind, this doesn't give a complete picture, as some of us will still have our mortgages during retirement while others will be done beforehand. It makes more sense to have your financial planner run your scenarios to retirement age so you can look clearly at the whole picture. This big-picture thinking is necessary to make the decision that's right for you.

THE EFFECT OF INTEREST RATES ON PREPAYMENTS

Two factors can impact the length of your mortgage: the amount you prepay and the interest rate of the mortgage. At a higher interest rate, we've seen that you save quite a bit of interest by making prepayments early on, and because those interest savings are quite large, you save more time. At a lower interest rate, the savings are less both in terms of the interest you save and the amount of time you save.

However, when your interest rate is lower, your mortgage would cost you less overall. Would you rather make extra payments toward something when it costs you less to do so or wait until the price tag goes up, just so your savings could be higher? When we say that we should only prepay when interest rates are high, we miss the point that when they are high, our total costs are higher.

I think that it's more important to look at the big picture, including the balance on your mortgage, your time to retirement, the amount you already have saved, and the amount you actually need during retirement. Prepayments can also help protect your budget from the impact of interest rate changes, which can be a very real problem, as Mom & Pop Average are about to find out.

A DOSE OF REALITY: RISING PAYMENT AMOUNTS

In a perfect world with static interest rates and rates of return, the calculations could be run like they always have been. But now you know better, so when you talk to your financial planner, be sure that they run projections for you showing at a 1% to 3%[76] interest rate increase on your mortgage each term. If rates don't increase that much, you'll have more to save or prepay; if they do, you will be prepared and able to handle the future. Let's see how this all works out for our happy families.

Mom & Pop Average

Let's take a look at what would happen to Mom & Pop Average's mortgage payments if they held their $450,000 mortgage through this period of time, using all the same assumptions as before.

GROSS FAMILY INCOME: $86,932					
YEAR	INTEREST RATE	PAYMENT	CUMULATIVE DIFFERENCE	BALANCE END TERM	CUMULATIVE INTEREST
1–5	3.96%	$ 2,357.34	$ 0.00	$ 391,469	$ 82,910
6–10	4.80%	$ 2,530.34	$ 173.00	$ 325,249	$ 168,510
11–15	5.60%	$ 2,663.73	$ 306.39	$ 245,046	$ 248,131
16–20	8.34%	$ 2,998.87	$ 641.53	$ 147,209	$ 330,226
21–25	10.60%	$ 3,154.86	$ 797.52	$ 0	$ 372,308

This is the same chart we saw in Chapter 1, with our history-in-reverse example. The payment ended up being $797.52

a month, or $9,570.24 a year more than when the mortgage began. In order to keep up with payments and not feel the strain, Mom & Pop Average's income would need to increase enough to offset the added costs. If it didn't, the money would have to come from somewhere, and any saving they had been doing would probably be the first thing to come off the list.

In this example, let's assume that Mom & Pop's salaries increase just enough to keep up with the cost of living. The kids grow up, become teenagers, and have increasing needs for food, clothing, and activities, so the family is only able to stay within their original contribution. As their mortgage payments become more expensive, they see the amount they have left to save decrease as follows:

YEAR	AMOUNT OF SAVINGS PER MONTH	END OF PERIOD RATE OF RETURN	
		4%	8%
1–5	$ 362.22	$ 24,015	$ 26,615
6–10	$ 189.22	$ 41,867	$ 53,555
11–15	$ 55.83	$ 54,821	$ 83,891
16–20	$ 0	$ 66,936	$ 124,985
21–25	$ 0	$ 81,729	$ 186,208

Now if Mom & Pop were comparing this with their original expectations of saving $362.22 a month for twenty-five years, they would find that they realized significantly different results.

% OF QUALIFYING INCOME	MONTHLY PAYMENT	EXPECTED RATE OF RETURN	
		4%	8%
5%	$ 362.22	$ 186,228	$ 344,480

In addition, Mom & Pop Average would now need to find an additional $641.53 a month between Year 16 and Year 20 of the mortgage and $797.52 for the remaining five years. That represents an additional $86,343 they would need to contribute over that ten-year period. If their income didn't increase enough to cover the difference, they may find themselves dipping into the savings they created, undoing the good work they had done up to that point. If they didn't have enough money saved, they may find themselves in the position of needing to refinance to keep their mortgage payments affordable. This would ultimately increase the total cost of the mortgage, lengthen it, and make it that much more difficult to save for retirement.

They ask their CFP Professional to test out three difference scenarios applying 5% of their qualifying income toward investing, prepayments, or both so they can see where the different actions would take them.

SCENARIO 1: Mom & Pop Average will not make any prepayments but will invest 5% of their income. As their mortgage payments increase over the years, the amount they are saving will decrease by the amount of the mortgage payment increase.

SCENARIO 2: Mom & Pop Average will use half of the 5% to prepay their mortgage and will invest the other half until rising interest rates stop their ability to save and prepay.

SCENARIO 3: Mom & Pop Average will apply the full 5% toward the mortgage.

In Scenarios #2 and #3, once the mortgage is paid, they will apply any money that would have otherwise gone toward the mortgage into their savings for the remainder of the twenty-five year period.

Here is what it looks like:

	SCENARIO 1	SCENARIO 2	SCENARIO 3
MORTGAGE: $ 450,000	**WITHOUT PREPAYMENT**	**50% PREPAYMENT 50% SAVINGS**	**5% PREPAYMENT**
Total Mortgage Payments	$ 822,308	$ 770,688	$ 730,267
Total Interest Cost	$ 372,308	$ 320,688	$ 280,267
Mortgage End	25 yrs	23 yrs, 2 mths	21 yrs, 8 mths
Interest Savings	$ 0	$ 51,620	$ 92,041
Investments with a 4% Rate of Return	$ 81,729	$ 112,755	$ 134,754
Investments with an 8% Rate of Return	$ 186,208	$ 167,592	$ 144,075

Now let's analyze the outcomes. In all three scenarios, the investing and/or prepayments initially stopped after Year 15 as the cost of the mortgage increased.

SCENARIO 1: Investment Results: If the money were just invested for the full twenty-five years, scenario 1 would have the best results with an annualized rate of return of 8% but the worst return of all three scenarios with a 4% rate of return. The 4% rate of return scenario with no prepayment showed the worst outcome of the bunch because the average interest rate on the mortgage was higher than the long-term rate of return. When interest rates increase, this will be an important thing to keep in mind. However, when the average investment rate of return was greater than the average mortgage rate with a consistent rate of return of 8%, the outcome was that a greater amount accumulated for the investor.

SCENARIO 2: Investment Results: The amount accumulated was neither the best nor the worst of the three scenarios. Additional saving of the amount that would have otherwise gone to the mortgage was invested after the mortgage ended in the last year and ten months. However, that left only a limited amount of time for the additional money to compound before it was required in Year 25.

Conservative investors may be more comfortable using a prepayment strategy, as there is less risk, as long as their amount of prepayment and time before retirement also showed that it made sense to do so. At this level of savings the time created was not enough to exceed the growth they could earn with a consistent 8% annual rate of return and no prepayment. However, if this family wanted a balanced approached at this level of savings, a different split between prepayments and investments could be the right solution. The actual amount of the split would be determined by the level of savings that they have, which has not been discussed in these examples.

SCENARIO 3: Investment Results: From a financial planner's point of view, this action is risky if Mom & Pop Average are retiring right when the mortgage comes up in Year 25 because they are heavily dependent on being able to invest a large amount of money in the last three years and four months before their retirement. If they don't have additional savings being made through their employer, they should not take this action in case life throws a curveball right before retirement and, for whatever reason, they are unable to save. It also showed the worst results of the 8% rate of return examples because the money was not given enough time to compound properly.

The difference in these three scenarios is largely due to effect of compounding, the level of savings, and the time that the prepayments create, which should all be thoroughly tested before a decision is made.

After seeing the impact of applying 5% of their income, Mom & Pop Average want to see the effects of applying 10% of their original qualifying income.

If Mom & Pop Average had used *The Debt-Free Lifestyle* system to create the equivalent of 10% of their income as free cash flow, it would cover the changes of interest rates for the first twenty years of the mortgage. However, if instead they were saving this 10% and their savings decreased as their mortgage payments increased, it would look like this:

GROSS INCOME: $ 86,932		10% PREPAYMENT PER MONTH: $ 724.44	
		END OF PERIOD RATE OF RETURN	
YEAR	AMOUNT OF SAVINGS PER MONTH	4%	8%
1–5	$ 724.44	$ 48,030	$ 53,229
6–10	$ 551.44	$ 95,204	$ 119,822
11–15	$ 418.05	$ 143,960	$ 209,233
16–20	$ 82.91	$ 181,271	$ 317,816
21–25	$ 0	$ 221,331	$ 473,497

Again, this is a different outcome from their original expectation based on 10% of the original qualifying income because as their mortgage payment increased over the years, they had less available to save.

		EXPECTED RATE OF RETURN	
% OF QUALIFYING INCOME	MONTHLY PAYMENT	4%	8%
10%	$724.44	$ 372,455	$ 688,960

They would again like to test the same three scenarios: no prepayment, a 50/50 split, and the full 10% going as a prepayment.

MORTGAGE: $450,000	SCENARIO 1 WITHOUT PREPAYMENT	SCENARIO 2 50% PREPAYMENT 50% SAVINGS	SCENARIO 3 10% PREPAYMENT
Total Mortgage Payments	$ 822,308	$ 712,602	$ 651,709
Total Interest Cost	$ 372,308	$ 262,602	$ 201,709
Mortgage End	25 yrs	20 yrs, 9 mths	17 yrs, 8 mths
Interest Savings	$ 0	$ 109,706	$ 170,599
Investments with a 4% Rate of Return	$ 221,331	$ 285,731	$ 319,405
Investments with an 8% Rate of Return	$ 473,497	$ 427,631	$ 372,635

SCENARIO 1: There were no prepayments. Instead, Mom & Pop Average invested until the increased mortgage payments ate up the 10% of their income they had allotted to savings, which occurred after Year 20.

Investment Results: Investments again performed the best of all three scenarios with an 8% rate of return and the worst of all scenarios with a 4% rate of return, showing the impact of compound interest.

SCENARIO 2: Half of the money went toward savings while the other half went into investments. After Year 20, saving stopped briefly until the mortgage finished, and then what had been the full mortgage payment was saved until Year 25.

Investment Results: Again scenario 2 had performance that showed a more balanced approach. However, perhaps the more important point is that compared to the previous example where only 5% of income was saved during an increasing interest rate environment, these examples where 10% is saved lead to a much more reliable retirement nest egg.

SCENARIO 3: The larger prepayments freed up a considerable amount of time, allowing the compounding at a lower rate to show the best results of the 4% rate of return examples. Perhaps the more important point is that because an additional 10% of the original qualifying income was already incorporated into the amount Mom & Pop Average were used to paying, they didn't have to deal with shocks to their budget from increased payments that would have otherwise occurred in the last ten years of their mortgage. Because of the higher amount they had available to prepay, their mortgage was completely done in Year 18, with interest savings of $170,559. With the mortgage done early, they would have completely avoided the higher payments in the last seven years, much to the relief of their cash flow, and wouldn't be in the position of having to refinance or dip into their savings to pay for the increased mortgage costs if they were unable to support the higher payment amount with their income.

Investment Results: Best of the 4% rate of return scenarios and worst of the 8% rate of return scenarios.

Mom & Pop Average now have an important decision to make. Looking at all three scenarios, they can see how a higher level of prepayment applied consistently during the first half of their mortgage can save a lot of interest and a lot of time. But achieving a consistently high rate of return on their investments can leave them with a higher amount in the savings account for retirement.

Which will be more important to them? Lowering their interests costs and shortening the time on the mortgage to minimize the shocks from interest rate increases? Or having a higher amount of money saved at retirement if they are more aggressive investors and the market cooperates? This is where Mom & Pop Average would also take a close look at any savings done through their employers. That would help to elevate their level of savings as well and would affect the decision of how much should go toward prepayment versus the investments.

Mr. Metro

Now in his fifties, Mr. Metro's biggest concern is getting ready for his retirement. Mr. Metro's employer has consistently been putting money into his pension plan for years. Mr. Metro has also found that he has 5% of his income available to prepay or to invest. His high income along with his aggressive investing style and the ten years he has remaining until his retirement has him leaning toward investing the money. However, he is concerned about his mortgage costs increasing during his retirement and would like to see how a limited amount of prepayments could help him manage his costs.

His first consideration is going to be based on how far along the amortization schedule he is. Due to his refinancing, he has taken a few steps backward over the years, which means prepayments are not as attractive. He is in Year 11 of the amortization schedule when he begins.

Second, with his high income, he could get a substantial amount of tax back if he made contributions into his RRSP, so that becomes a compelling argument in favour of investing.

Third, because of his pension and savings over the years, Mr. Metro already has a large amount saved. If the growth he could earn investing over the next ten years is greater than the interest savings from prepayments, he should consider that.

Mr. Metro asks his CFP Professional to run the following test which has him making prepayments from Year 11 to Year 15.

MORTAGE BALANCE OUTSTANDING	NO PREPAYMENT	PREPAY NEXT 5 YEARS
End of Year 15	$ 544,545	$ 492,572
Interest Saved	$ 0	$ 33,080
PROJECTED MORTGAGE PAYMENTS		
Year 16–20 (8.34% Interest Rate)	$ 6,664.14	$ 6,028.09
Year 21–25 (10.60% Interest Rate)	$ 7,010.75	$ 6,341.63

If Mr. Metro were to apply 5% of his income, or $753.85 per month, as a prepayment for the next five years, and then extend the mortgage for the remainder of a twenty-five year amortization period, he could potentially lower the amount of his mortgage payment during retirement. Not only would he save $33,080 in interest but he would also protect his payments from future rate increases by lowering the mortgage balance outstanding. If interest rates increased more modestly than projected, or decreased, he would still have a lower payment to sustain. Alternatively, if he made the same amount of pre-payments for five years and then continued with the normal payment schedule, he would save $76,787 in interest. This becomes food for thought when he looks at the amount he has available in his retirement budget. Mr. Metro would then compare these results to the amount he already has accumulated in his investments to determine which outcome is best for him.

If Mr. Metro wanted to apply a higher percentage of his income to this program, he would have results comparable to Mom & Pop Average. However, if managing cash flow during retirement is a bigger concern, making prepayments—even only for five years—can help make his debt more manageable during retirement.

THE CORRECT ANSWER IS THE ONE THAT'S RIGHT FOR YOU

You now have the tools in your hands to choose what works for you, based on your own unique circumstances.

Using *The Debt-Free Lifestyle* system, you can:

- Pay off your consumer debt.

- Create a lifestyle that allows for regular savings and/or prepayments.
- Determine how much you can save with the simple budget.
- Determine how much you'll need for the future with the simple retirement budget.
- Save for the future all along.
- Prepay and save time and money on your mortgage.
- Use the time you created to amp up your savings for retirement.
- Retire happily ever after!

EXERCISE
YOUR POWER
TO CHOOSE

When we first met in the Introduction, I told you my real-world personal story about a humble financial planner and her spouse looking for a way to create a better life for themselves. It still rings true today, as I see clients just like us who are looking for a way to use their limited resources to make a good life and a comfortable future for themselves and the ones they love. They come from all walks of life, often overwhelmed. Most deal with it by trying not to think about it very often, but the weight of the world seems to lift off their shoulders when they discover, as we did, that there is a solution.

It all comes down to choice. It's the big decisions and the budget decisions you make on a daily basis that will determine your future. The big decisions—from where to live, the size of your mortgage, your transportation and work commute to the type of work you do—make up the largest part of your budget and have maximum impact. They will determine how much money you have left to spend on your smaller budget decisions. If you've made big decisions that don't fit into your overall financial plan, you can change them, but it may be difficult. That is why it's so important to make these choices with a solid understanding of what you can actually afford and how well your budget can handle changing economic circumstances like a rise in interest rates. If you get the big decisions right, you'll be able to decide how much of your income is available to further your financial goals, such as prepaying your mortgage or saving for retirement, and you'll have enough left over to make smart budget decisions. Whether you use the simple budget system like we do or have a different budgeting system that works for you, make sure you use it frequently and consistently. Please find a CFP Professional to help you through this process so you don't make these decisions alone.

Our story ends with a small balance still owing on our mortgage, but it is only a matter of time before it is paid off. Then, without the pressure of making a mortgage payment each month, Cameron will be able to quit his job at the post office and pursue writing full-time. He'd like to build a business around the work he does and will have the freedom to do so. I've since been made a partner in my financial planning firm and am happy continuing with what I'm doing. I'm more passionate than ever about educating people about personal finance and helping them along the way as they make their own decisions around finances and life choices. Now in our early thirties, Cameron and I have plenty of time to save. We've created a lifestyle that we can enjoy and are comfortable with.

Mom & Pop Average and Mr. Metro have graciously joined us on this debt-free journey. While a real Mom & Pop Average do not exist, they are a representation of the parents I've met over the years. Having a workable budgeting process in place is even more important to them as they have the costs associated with raising a young family. They are enjoying their new house. Since their mortgage is brand new, they have seen the advantages of redirecting some of the extra money they found in their budget toward principal prepayments—especially while the bulk of each payment in the traditional amortization schedule is going toward interest. By being proactive about it, they feel they are making progress. They really like the idea of going into retirement without a mortgage, and once the kids have moved out, and the mortgage is paid, they plan to live modestly and may even downsize to take some of the money out of the house. They are working with a financial planner, who has helped them figure out how to balance their savings for retirement with the prepayments, given their timeline.

Because of the refinancing Mr. Metro has done over the years, he realized that he slid backward on the amortization schedule a few times and has paid more interest than he would've liked—increasing the total cost of his already expensive home. He worked out a retirement budget and took careful inventory of his spending habits and current level of savings. He learned that his pension plan should be able to cover the majority of his fixed expenses during retirement, and that if he makes better budget decisions he will be able to save enough money before he retires to help cover his mortgage payments for the remaining years. Since he wants to retire in the next ten years, he is mostly concerned with having enough money to comfortably retire. Because he is further along in his amortization schedule and because of the amount he has already saved, the prepayments are not as attractive as they would have been early on. The tax paid on his higher income generates a generous tax refund if he invests in his RRSPs, and he likes the idea of getting back the money now that would have otherwise gone to taxes and paying taxes when he has a much lower income during retirement. He decides to redirect the rest of his money into savings for retirement since he now knows that he can support his mortgage payments during retirement. He likes the simple budget, which allows him to put aside a little extra spending money some weeks at his discretion to take Junior out to a hockey game or for a dinner so they can really enjoy their last couple years of living together before Junior moves out on his own.

WHAT ARE YOUR FINANCIAL PRIORITIES?

It can feel a bit like work to apply the simple budget system every time you get paid in order to determine the amount you can direct toward your financial goals. And granted, making big decisions that serve you well both now and in the future can be challenging because it goes against our consumer mentality of wanting the best and wanting it now! The process that Cam and I have gone through is very much an exercise in delayed gratification. But the truth is, with the cost of living ever on the rise, our choices today will determine our level of comfort in the future.

Cam and I have already made our decisions, and it has resulted in over $150,000 going toward our debt in the past six years. We could have gone the traditional route like everyone else. Had we done so, we would still have nineteen years to go on our mortgage. Because we started young, we'll still have thirty years to save our money—mortgage-free—before it will be time for us to retire.

How has making the conventional choices served you? The biggest impact you can have on your budget is making long-term choices that are right for you and that create free cash flow to accelerate your success. But perhaps even more important is choosing to structure your debt repayment so that you are paying down more principal and getting a step closer to debt freedom. If you make no other choice than to take advantage of the structure of your debts, like the amortization schedule on your mortgage, you will still be ahead of the game. However, there will come a time when interest rates go on the rise again. Then the work you are doing now will really shine, as you will have saved yourself more in total payments and total interest over the lifetime of your mortgage. Prepayments at that time will become more important than ever to ensure that the money going into your house isn't lost as interest paid to the lender, and that the increase payments that you'll be making won't be costing your future.

The decisions we make have ripple effects throughout our whole lives. The bigger the price tag, the more of an influence it will have on your financial well-being. It is far easier to have our biggest decisions line up with our lifetime objectives than it is to try to scrimp and squeeze out a lifestyle when the decisions don't fit. We all have only so much disposable income, and if you've purchased a home that will prove to be more than you can afford over the long-term, your best defence is paying down the principal while you still have the flexibility in your budget to do so. Regardless of what you choose, having the information about how prepayments, interest rates, and the amortization schedule all work together puts the control back in your hands. You now have the ability to see the impact of the decisions you are making. A little extra cash flow can go a long way. You now have the power to choose what you will do next.

So before you put this book down, ask yourself, What is my financial priority? Is it debt freedom, like it was for us? Is it finishing the mortgage so that you can focus on saving for retirement? Once you've chosen your goal, the best investment that you can make is hiring a CFP professional that you trust to work with you thoroughout the years and hold you accountable. Then, make a commitment to yourself and your future self that you're willing to do what it takes to achieve it.

notes

1 http://www.ctvnews.ca/canada/median-family-income-in-canada-is-76-000-statscan-survey-shows-1.1449641.

2 http://www.livingwageforfamilies.ca/about/living-wages-in-bc-canada/; http://www.livingwageforfamilies.ca/what_is_living_wage; http://www.livingwagecanada.ca/files/7813/8243/8036/living_wage_full_document.pdf; http://www.huffingtonpost.ca/2015/04/29/living-wage-metro-vancouver_n_7173058.html.

3 http://www.statcan.gc.ca/pub/75-001-x/2012002/article/11636/11636hl-fs-eng.htm.

4 http://www.pbo-dpb.gc.ca/web/default/files/Documents/Reports/2016/Household%20Debt/Household_Debt_EN.pdf.

5 http://www.theglobeandmail.com/report-on-business/economy/canadians-household-debt-to-hit-new-record-this-year-report-says/article28254553/.

6 http://www.fraserinstitute.org/sites/default/files/longer-term-perspective-on-canadas-household-debt.pdf.

7 Louis Hyman, *Borrow: The American Way of Debt* (New York: Vintage Books, 2012).

8 Ibid.

9 Louis Hyman, *Borrow: The American Way of Debt* (New York: Vintage Books, 2012).

10 http://www.fraserinstitute.org/sites/default/files/longer-termperspective-on-canadas-household-debt.pdf.

11 http://cfs-fcee.ca/wp-content/uploads/sites/2/2013/05/Factsheet-2015-05-Private-Student-Debt-EN.pdf.

12 http://cfs-fcee.ca/wp-content/uploads/sites/2/2015/03/Report-Impact-of-Student-Debt-2015-Final.pdf.

13 http://www.transunioninsights.ca/MarketTrends/.

14 https://newsroom.bmo.com/press-releases/bmo-annual-debt-report-interest-rate-rise-would-i-tsx-bmo-201507101016484001.

15 http://www.fcac-acfc.gc.ca/Eng/resources/publications/yourRights/Documents/RightRespCC-eng.pdf.

16 http://www.investopedia.com/terms/p/primerate.asp.

17 https://www03.cmhc-schl.gc.ca/catalog/productDetail.cfm?cat=63&itm=1&lang=en&sid=qezYiNfxszXrRvKg4rC9FwAdJHR7khxA3e5L7RtDl8FYlednBgOYINNUPQ6xpWb3&fr=1442110502489.

18 http://www.fcac-acfc.gc.ca/Eng/resources/publications/mortgages/Pages/home-accueil.aspx.

19 http://cmhc.ca/en/co/index.cfm.

20 David Baxter, Stanley W. Hamilton, and Daniel D. Ulinder, "Mortgage Underwriting and Residential Borrower Qualification," in *Real Estate Finance in a Canadian Context* (Vancouver: UBC Real Estate Division, 2013).

21 David Baxter, Stanley W. Hamilton, and Daniel D. Ulinder, *Real Estate Finance in a Canadian Context* (Vancouver: UBC Real Estate Division, 2013).

22 http://www.bankofcanada.ca/wp-content/uploads/2013/12/fsr-december13-crawford.pdf.

23 http://laws-lois.justice.gc.ca/PDF/I-15.pdf.

24 http://www.manulifebank.ca/wps/portal/bankca/Bank.caHome/Bankingwithus/debt%20research/!ut/p/b1/hZLdkmtAFIWfJQ9gNE2MS_E3hPbXBDcqJKRJEAwmTz-TU6fqXJ3MvttV315Va61Np3RMp-1xJtVxIl17vD73dJvZ5m4HNZ4DOpY1YFiWraiMyzgO-wMkLwAd_nZ_oGO3WC1lNBZFjf3hgIMiMo6-sjb6GdpjCAJ1n95rVFEtuNttJ4CT

C4nGmPlQ9ry8axl_IrmMYejrwIgFkomjQ-FkEtBx_mSTUmpGZgJVC
O8zh-NcNQJW1MqtpZcNv0jpJSCKFNQflcyNC1HXbNnvSD1vy4Hy
2HCNqM-_HsF_RgK_eTTplOS3t6W4vYG3LceJPC8wDMOyUAQCHd
XJVnz6Vw1UmsUnQsr5MZa21J_Gqxte1Kz3it5axEtgNIjk-XiLxPPktSZ
jsZUhi-K7njuoKqS0SMLKHlFBSfbSmt1Drh5hw5FUOKcXVZQu_T4C
M5KheFy0kwcFD6E57ruhi3tWGKj3VY-cWI_2EGeCBtAdcAOZ7K8o7I
aP7rGcJvl6sHD4pa0OnzmHhMoySqNcZdlpJFOHZbP56TN9GcfzI_4
AL-JMfgDhnwKA0VMBWr7jeACEkMZ0DLgsqL9649E8_FoIFmw5A
FnJYlsqwFYCsBJArPJm0FwRCrk1qH2EsbeCQmQizVMlN-9B02xo9N
HdznR_C2eLnwP3NlffYcLexA!!/dl4/d5/L2dBISEvZ0FBIS9nQSEh/.

25 http://www.crea.ca/housing-market-stats/national-average-price-map/.

26 http://www.trebhome.com/market_news/market_watch/;
http://www.trebhome.com/market_news/market_watch/2016/
mw1602.pdf.

27 http://www.trebhome.com/market_news/market_watch/2016/
mw1601.pdf.

28 http://www.surrey.ca/city-services/593.aspx.

29 https://www.nrcan.gc.ca/energy/publications/efficiency/heating-
heat-pump/6835#table2.

30 http://www.winnipegassessment.com/AsmtTax/English/Property/
TaxRates.stm.

31 http://www.winnipegfreepress.com/templates/Tax_Calc.

32 http://www1.toronto.ca/wps/portal/contentonly?vgnextoid=63b0ff0
e43db1410VgnVCM10000071d60f89RCRD.

33 http://wx.toronto.ca/inter/fin/tax.nsf/tax?OpenForm&Seq=1.

34 https://www.cmhc-schl.gc.ca/en/hoficlincl/moloin/mupr/
mupr_015.cfm

35 GDSR of 35% used, based on current CMHC schedule.

36 Mortgage Brokerage in British Columbia Course, UBC, Sauder School
of Business, Real Estate Division, 2016.

37 http://laws-lois.justice.gc.ca/eng/regulations/SOR-2012-281/page-1.
html#docCont.

38 http://homeownership.ca/wp-content/uploads/2015/04/digest/en/
index.html.

[39] Calculations done via FP Solutions software, using monthly payment amounts and semi-annual compounding.

[40] http://www.osfi-bsif.gc.ca/Eng/fi-if/rg-ro/gdn-ort/gl-ld/Pages/b20.aspx.

[41] http://www.bankofcanada.ca/wp-content/uploads/2013/12/fsr-december13-crawford.pdf.

[42] http://laws-lois.justice.gc.ca/PDF/SOR-2012-281.pdf.

[43] http://www.ratehub.ca/best-mortgage-rates/5-year/fixed.

[44] http://www.bankofcanada.ca/rates/interest-rates/selected-historical-interest-rates/.

[45] http://www.fcac-acfc.gc.ca/eng/resources/publications/mortgages/Pages/BuyingYo-Acheterv-12.aspx.

[46] http://www.manulifebank.ca/wps/portal/bankca/Bank.caHome/Bankingwithus/debt%20research/!ut/p/b1/hZLdkmtAFIWfJQ9gN E2MS_E3hPbXBDcqJKRJEAwmTz-TU6fqXJ3MvttV315Va61Np3RMp-1xJtVxIl17vD73dJvZ5m4HNZ4DOpY1YFiWraiMyzgO-wMkLwAd_n Z_oGO3WC1lNBZFjf3hgIMiMo6-sjb6GdpjCAJ1n95rVFEtuNttJ4CTC4 nGmPlQ9ry8axl_IrmMYejrwIgFkomjQ-FkEtBx_mSTUmpGZgJVCO8 zh-NcNQJW1MqtpZcNv0jpJSCKFNQflcyNC1HXbNnvSD1vy4Hy2H CNqM-_HsF_RgK_eTTplOS3t6W4vYG3LceJPC8wDMOyUAQCHdXJ Vnz6Vw1UmsUnQsr5MZa21J_Gqxte1Kz3it5axEtgNIjk-XiLxPPktSZjs ZUhi-K7njuoKqS0SMLKHlFBSfbSmt1Drh5hw5FUOKcXVZQu_T4CM 5KheFy0kwcFD6E57ruhi3tWGKj3VY-cWI_2EGeCBtAdcAOZ7K8o7Ia P7rGcJvl6sHD4pa0OnzmHhMoySqNcZdlpJFOHZbP56TN9GcfzI_4A L-JMfgDhnwKA0VMBWr7jeACEkMZ0DLgsqL9649E8_FoIFmw5AFn JYlsqwFYCsBJArPJm0FwRCrk1qH2EsbeCQmQizVMlN-9B02xo9NH dznR_C2eLnwP3NlffYcLexA!!/dl4/d5/L2dBISEvZ0FBIS9nQSEh/.

[47] http://www.tradingeconomics.com/canada/personal-savings.

[48] https://www.cpacanada.ca/en/connecting-and-news/news/professional-news/2015/March/Household-finances-Canadians-at-risk.

[49] http://laws-lois.justice.gc.ca/eng/regulations/SOR-2012-281/page-1.html#docCont.

[50] http://www.huffingtonpost.ca/2015/04/29/living-wage-metro-vancouver_n_7173058.html.

[51] Mortgage Brokerage in British Columbia Course, UBC, Sauder School of Business, Real Estate Division, 2016.

[52] http://www.osfi-bsif.gc.ca/eng/docs/ar-ra/1213/eng/p2-eng.html.

[53] http://www.cmhc-schl.gc.ca/en/co/moloin/moloin_005.cfm.

[54] Mortgage Brokerage in British Columbia Course, UBC, Sauder School of Business, Real Estate Division, 2016.

[55] http://www.ratehub.ca/cmhc-mortgage-insurance.

[56] http://www.canadiancapitalist.com/mortgage-insurance-versus-life-insurance.

[57] http://www.cbc.ca/marketplace/episodes/2008-episodes/in-denial; https://www.thestar.com/opinion/columnists/2009/03/21/couples_story_offers_lesson_in_life_insurance.html.

[58] Mortgage Brokerage in British Columbia Course, UBC, Sauder School of Business, Real Estate Division, 2016.

[59] http://www.cmhc-schl.gc.ca/en/hoficlincl/moloin/mupr/mupr_015.cfm.

[60] www.statcan.gc.ca/pub/75-001-x/2012002/article/11636-eng.pdf.

[61] http://www.taxtips.ca/priortaxrates/taxrates2009_2010/bc.htm.

[62] http://www.cra-arc.gc.ca/tx/ndvdls/tpcs/ncm-tx/rtrn/cmpltng/ddctns/lns300-350/300-eng.html.

[63] http://www.taxtips.ca/calculators/basic/basic-tax-calculator.htm.

[64] http://www.taxtips.ca/calculators/basic/basic-tax-calculator.htm.

[65] http://www.pbo-dpb.gc.ca/web/default/files/Documents/Reports/2016/Household%20Debt/Household_Debt_EN.pdf.

[66] http://www.statcan.gc.ca/pub/75-006-x/2014001/article/14120-eng.pdf; http://www.statcan.gc.ca/tables-tableaux/sum-som/l01/cst01/labor26a-eng.htm.

[67] http://www.tradingeconomics.com/canada/personal-savings.

[68] http://careers.workopolis.com/advice/job-hopping-is-the-new-normal/.

[69] https://www.sunlife.ca/ca/Insurance/Health+insurance/Long+term+care+insurance/5+stages+of+care?vgnLocale=en_CA.

[70] https://www.fcm.ca/Documents/reports/FCM/No_Vacancy_Trends_in_Rental_Housing_in_Canada_EN.pdf.

[71] http://www2.gov.bc.ca/gov/content/housing-tenancy/residential-tenancies/during-a-tenancy/rent-increases; http://www2.gov.bc.ca/assets/gov/housing-and-tenancy/residential-tenancies/policy-guidelines/gl37.pdf.

[72] http://creastats.crea.ca/natl/index.htm.

[73] Ibid.

[74] http://www.taxtips.ca/stocksandbonds/investmentreturns.htm.

[75] http://www.fpsc.ca/docs/default-source/FPSC/projection-assumption-guidelines.pdf.

[76] http://www.canadianmortgagetrends.com/mortgage-stress-tester.

Note: The charts on pp. 107 and 109 were run using Wolters Kluwer, FP Solutions http://connect.cch.ca/LP=2032?LeadSource=FPVideo-Adwords&utm_campaign=fpsolutions&utm_medium=cpc&utm_source=FPVideo-Adwords&gclid=CMO3_rH30M4CFUSBfgodICgOvw.

about the author

Christine Conway, CFP®, CHS, is a financial planner specializing in debt and retirement who practices primarily in the Lower Mainland, B.C. She loves the work that she does and enjoys being able to help people better understand their finances and achieve their financial goals.

Christine joined Braun Financial Services Ltd. as a financial advisor in July 2009 and became a partner in the firm on November 28, 2014. Prior to working at Braun Financial Services, Christine spent four years between two managing general agencies, supporting advisors as they worked with various insurance and investment products. Christine holds the Certified Financial Planner (CFP®) designation, Certified

Health Insurance Specialist (CHS) designation, a Bachelor of Arts from Providence College as well as an Associate Customer Service designation from LOMA, the Life Office Management Association. She is also passionate about giving back to the community. She served on the board of directors for the New Westminster Chamber of Commerce from February 2011 to June 2016, and as chair of the board from February 2013 to April 2015. She remains actively involved in the New Westminster community. Outside of the office, Christine enjoys hiking and spending time with her husband, Cameron.